AGING AND DISABILITIES: SEEKING COMMON GROUND

Edward F. Ansello
and
Nancy N. Eustis, Editors

GENERATIONS AND AGING SERIES

Originally published as the Winter 1992 issue of *GENERATIONS,* Journal of the American Society on Aging, Mary Johnson, Editor.

Routledge
Taylor & Francis Group
LONDON AND NEW YORK

Originally published 1992 by The American Society on Aging and Baywood Publishing Company, Inc.

Published 2018 by Routledge
2 Park Square, Milton Park, Abingdon, Oxon OX14 4RN
52 Vanderbilt Avenue, New York, NY 10017

First issued in hardback 2018

Routledge is an imprint of the Taylor & Francis Group, an informa business

Library of Congress Catalog Number: 92-28829

Library of Congress Cataloging-in-Publication Data

Aging and disabilities : seeking common ground / Edward F. Ansello and Nancy N. Eustis, editors.
p. cm. – – (Generations and aging series)
"Originally published as the Winter 1992 issue of Generations, journal of the American Society on Aging."
ISBN 0-89503-108-6
1. Developmentally disabled aged- -Services for- -United States. 2. Aged- -Services for- -United States. I. Ansello, Edward F. II. Eustis, Nancy N., 1941- . III. Generations (San Francisco, Calif.) IV. Series.
HV3009.5.A35A37 1992
362.4'084'6- -dc20 92-28829
CIP

ISBN 13: 978-0-415-78515-0 (hbk)
ISBN 13: 978-0-89503-108-2 (pbk)

Table of Contents

Chapter

1 A Common Stake? Investigating the Emerging 'Intersection' of Aging and Disabilities
Edward F. Ansello and Nancy N. Eustis 1

SEEKING COMMON GROUND

2 Seeking Common Ground Between Aging and Developmental Disabilities
Edward F. Ansello 9

3 Common Needs, Different Solutions? Younger and Older Homecare Clients
Nancy N. Eustis and Lucy Rose Fischer 25

REHABILITATION SERVICES FOR ELDERS

4 Aging and Rehabilitation: Beyond the Medical Model
Stanley J. Brody and Malcolm H. Morrison 39

5 Geriatric Rehabilitation
Kenneth Brummel-Smith 47

6 Availability of Rehabilitation Services for Elders: A Study of Critical Policy and Financing Issues
Linda A. Wray and Fernando M. Torres-Gil 55

7 What Are We Trying to Restore? A Case for Habilitation
Paul A. Raia 69

8 The Kona Adult Day Center: Rehabilitation in Adult Daycare
Karen L. Klemme 75

INDEPENDENT LIVING IN THE COMMUNITY

9 Independent Living and Community Life: Building Coalitions Among Elders, People with Disabilities, and Our Allies
Julie Ann Racino and Judith E. Heumann 79

10 What Is Independence?
Elias S. Cohen 91

11 Consumer-Directed Homecare: What Makes It Possible?
Charles P. Sabatino and Simi Litvak 99

12 Adjusting to Early- and Late-Onset Disability: A Personal Perspective
Jean B. Zink 111

13 Planning for the Transfer of Care
Joan B. Wood and Laura Lopater Skiles 115

14 'Retirement' for Older Persons with Developmental Disabilities
Evelyn Sutton, Harvey L. Sterns, and Ruth S. Roberts 121

EDUCATION AND TRAINING FOR INDEPENDENT LIVING

15 Training Families to Be Case Managers for Elders with Developmental Disabilities
Marsha Mailick Seltzer 127

16 The Training of a Specialist in Developmental Disabilities and Aging
Evelyn Sutton, Harvey L. Sterns, Lisa Schwartz, and Ruth Roberts 139

17 Aging with a Disability: Educating Myself
June Isaacson Kailes 149

A UNIFIED POLITICAL AGENDA?

18 Autonomy as a Policy Goal for Disability and Aging
Laurel Beedon 157

19 Aging, Disability, and Long-Term Care: The Politics of Common Ground
Robert H. Binstock 165

20 The Independent Living Model of Personal Assistance in National Long-Term-Care Policy
Gerben DeJong, Andrew I. Batavia, and Louise Bouscaren McKnew 177

21 Changing Complex Long-Term-Care Systems
Kay Charron 193

Chapter 1

A Common Stake? Investigating the Emerging 'Intersection' of Aging and Disabilities

Edward F. Ansello and
Nancy N. Eustis

The separation of aging and disability has been axiomatic in gerontology for the past three decades. Even before this, in the development of national social insurance programs, the two were separated politically, the result being that passage of disability insurance lagged behind old age insurance by 21 years. Not surprisingly, the "systems" of researchers, advocates, and service providers that grew up around each constituency have had little history of meaningful interaction with each other.

While the dissociation of aging and disability may be technically correct in that aging does not equal disability, and vice verse, more adults than ever before are either experiencing disabilities in old age or aging through life with disabilities. Approximately one American in seven (35 million persons) has a physical or mental impairment that interferes with daily activities (Institute of Medicine, 1991). The likelihood of disability increases with age. While some 7 percent of those under 18 years of age are limited in activity, in fair or poor health, or both, about 48 percent of persons age 65 and above fall into one of these three categories (Ries and Brown, 1991).

In this volume we investigate the emerging "intersection" of aging and disabilities, focusing upon elders with disabilities and younger adults with developmental or other types of disabilities who are approaching retirement age. Our purpose is to examine these individuals and highlight four systems (aging, developmental disabilities, independent living movement, and rehabilitation) that serve them, in order to explore their common stake.

UNPRECEDENTED NUMBERS OF LIFELONG AND LATE-ONSET DISABILITIES

A *lifelong impairment* is codified (Public Law 101-496) as a developmental disability (DD) when it is attributable to mental or physical impairments, or a combination of both, that become manifest before age 22; is likely to continue indefinitely; results in substantial functional limitations in three or more areas of major life activity, such as self-care, language, learning, mobility, self-direction, economic self-sufficiency, and capacity for independent living; and requires lifelong or extended services. Developmental disabilities *may* include cerebral palsy, mental retardation, autism, blindness and deafness, but the definition is functional, not categorical. In the recent past, such developmental disabilities meant a relatively short life expectancy, and there was thus no reason for the broad aging network to be involved. For example, the estimated life expectancy of a person with mental retardation was about 35 to 45 years during the 1960s (Janicki and Wisniewski, 1985). Now, in numbers without precedent, adults with lifelong developmental disabilities are surviving into old age and, in many instances, are outliving their parents, who have been providing informal support for them (Rose and Ansello, 1987).

The total number of older Americans with developmental disabilities is debated. First, being primarily community dwellers rather than institutional residents and typically receiving no formal services or programs, they are not figured in agency "counts." Second, and perhaps more important, number estimates are complicated by disagreements on who is under or wants to be under the DD umbrella, which, by default and by virtue of the large core of its clients and professionals, has been dominated by those in and concerned for mental retardation. Other networks have distanced themselves from the developmental disabilities service system's perceived emphasis upon brain dysfunction therefore, estimates by mental retardation/developmental disabilities professionals (e.g., Janicki, 1991) of about 4 of every 1,000 people above age 60 having developmental disabilities might reasonably be considered very conservative. Our own estimate (Ansello and

Rose, 1989) of about 1 in 100 elders attempts to take this into account. Further, we expect this number to double, perhaps to triple, in the next 15 years as more community-dwelling elders, considered developmentally disabled prior to the 1950s, are discovered in two-generation geriatric families. This is likely to happen where the caregiving mainstream elder has died or become frail and the situation is called to the attention of the aging system. "Pre-1950s" is an important criterion because labels like "mentally retarded" were more frequently applied before 1950 for reasons unacceptable or unlikely today, such as behavior considered unruly or because of inadequate screening for such things as hearing loss or other physical causes of "abnormal" behavior. As a result, people labeled developmentally disabled who have survived to late life today include large numbers of relatively high functioning, less disabled adults. They also include those whose mislabeling may have meant institutionalization, socialization to a retardation system, and separation from the mainstream of education and community life. In addition, there are increasing numbers of adults surviving to middle age and older who are disabled because of such conditions as polio (including postpolio syndrome) and multiple sclerosis or traumatic injuries such as spinal cord and closed-head injuries. Because many of these individuals experienced the onset of their disabilities before the legal criterion of age 22, they contribute to the overall numbers of persons with lifelong developmental disabilities.

Late-onset impairments are increasingly a factor in late life. While 82 percent of all the members of the population covered in the National Health Interview Survey (NHIS) are not limited in activity and are in good-to-excellent health, disability, defined as limitations in activity and respondent-assessed fair or poor health status, is much more likely with greater age (LaPlante, 1989; Ries and Brown, 1991). For example, using the NHIS Home Care Supplement, 1979-80, LaPlante (1989) identified 3.3 persons per 1,000 aged 18-44, 37.5 per 1,000 aged 65-74, and 89.2 per 1,000 aged 75-84 as needing assistance in walking. Similar comparisons of the need for assistance in using the toilet and assistance with eating, both less common than the need for assistance in walking, showed 22 times and 15 times the need, comparing youngest and oldest groups. Limitation in activity has been found to be associated with fair or poor health status for elders, and vice versa (Ries and Brown, 1991). Both, in turn, are associated with advanced age.

Today there are approximately 6.5 million persons over age 65 with chronic vision impairments or blindness; the majority of all blind and visually impaired Americans are adults who lost their vision after becoming elderly. Some 9.5 million persons over age 65 have hearing impairments or deafness, with projections of 11.0 million by the end of this decade. About 6.0 million elders have communication impairments. The estimates of elders with Alzheimer's disease or other forms of dementia keep climbing. There are unknown millions of elders with multiple impairments, and survival to later life now means increasing numbers of older adults with late-onset impairments overlaying lifelong impairments. One example is seen with the growing recognition of Alzheimer's disease among older adults with Down's syndrome (Ansello, 1988).

PREVIOUS LINKAGES BETWEEN AGING AND DISABILITIES

In the years since *Generations* published its Summer 1984 issue, "The Disabled Older Person," there have been three notable explorations of common ground between persons with early-onset disabilities and those who serve them, on the one hand, and those who have late-onset disabilities and their service system, on the other.

1. *Aging and rehabilitation.* While the discipline of physical medicine and rehabilitation has traditionally been quite separate from the discipline of geriatric medicine, their clients are drawing them together—those with disabilities are growing older, and more elders have disabilities. Brody and others have convened two conferences of experts in geriatrics and in rehabilitation (Brody and Ruff, 1986; Brody and Pawlson, 1990) to discuss what they can learn from each other. The results include an emphasis on function rather than diagnosis in describing abilities of persons with disabilities and recognition of the need for training professionals in both rehabilitation and geriatrics.

2. *Aging and independent living.* Under the leadership of the World Institute on Disability and the Center for Health and Aging at the University of California in San Francisco, the aging and disability communities have met together to discuss the possibility of "a unified agenda" (Mahoney et al., 1986). These and other discussions (e.g., Simon-Rusinowitz, 1991) have explored common concerns, including social stigmas imposed on individuals with disabilities and inadequate health and personal assistance services. Younger persons with disabilities are concerned about the qualities and characteristics of programs available for elders with disabilities.

3. *Aging and developmental disabilities.* The 1987 Wingspread Conference on Aging and Lifelong Disabilities, which drew together leaders from the aging and mental retardation/developmental disabilities systems, seems to have been pivotal in stimulating cooperative efforts. Since then, leaders from these fields have developed joint training initiatives, participated in each other's annual meetings, sponsored national and international conferences, published monographs and issues of journals, and assisted each other in the passage of federal and state legislation affecting aging and developmental disabilities. Notable accomplishments include successful advocacy for specific attention to aging and to disabilities in the 1987 amendments to the Developmental Disabilities Assistance and Bill of Rights Act and the Older Americans Act, respectively.

OVERVIEW OF THIS VOLUME

This volume addresses the extent to which younger and older adults with disabilities have common needs and interests, and the extent to which they and persons who work with them can learn from each other and join forces in arriving at shared solutions. There are a number of obstacles, such as differences in priorities, funding formulas, language, and practices. Potentially, a tension exists between the structured dependency characteristic of much of the aging system and the assertive control by clients characteristic of the independent living movement, with geriatric rehabilitation perhaps representing a blend of professional and self-advocacy. We discuss this tension in some detail throughout this volume. The issue includes thoughtful essays and also highlights exemplary programs that will help the reader to understand better the intersection of aging and disabilities.

Chapters in the first section, "Seeking Common Ground," discuss efforts by two communities or systems to explore what they can learn from each other. Ansello describes fruitful initiatives that bring together the aging and developmental disabilities systems. Eustis compares the needs of younger and older persons with disabilities, and the service strategies of the aging network and independent living movement. Brody and Morrison review change in aging and healthcare interventions that result in an emphasis on enhancing functioning and an evolution in the purpose of rehabilitation.

In the section on "Rehabilitation Services for the Elderly," Brummel-Smith explicates the principles of geriatric rehabilitation. Presenting results from a survey of congressional staff persons and state agency personnel, Wray and Torres-Gil identify barriers to more common provision of rehabilitation to older persons. Raia and Klemme, respectively, discuss practical adaptations required of the rehabilitation model when employed with older persons with visual impairments and Alzheimer's disease and describe productive applications of rehabilitation in a geriatric daycare setting.

"Independent Living in the Community" is a common goal of the aging and developmental disabilities service systems as well as of the independent living movement. Chapters in the third section discuss varying perspectives on this shared goal and approaches to achieving it. Cohen suggests that autonomy and independent must be gauged from the client's perspective. Two of the chapters link coauthors from different systems: Racino (developmental disabilities) and Heumann (independent living movement); Sabatino (aging) and Litvak (independent living movement). Zink, Wood, and Sutton et al. describe several characteristics of life with lifelong disabilities.

The fourth section relates insights in "Education and Training for Independent Living." Sutton and colleagues describe training of professionals who serve older persons with developmental disabilities, Seltzer reports on a program that trains family members to be case managers, and Kailes chronicles her own efforts to cope with growing older with a lifelong disability.

Contributors to the final section, "A Unified Political Agenda?," assess the political and policy substructure necessary to achieve common goals. Beedon identifies fundamental policy differences between the disabilities and aging communities. Binstock analyzes how the constituencies perceive a supposedly shared objective, enactment of a national health insurance program. DeJong et al. examine what must be done to institute a national personal assistance program, a goal of the independent living movement, and Charron details the paradigm shifts that must take place in order to have a state program serving persons of all ages with disabilities.

OMISSIONS

It is important to note that the topic "aging and disabilities" is multifaceted. It can be approached in many ways. We have chosen to focus on four systems and areas of potential common ground. We have not addressed mental illness and aging. Moreover, there are other equally important areas of shared concern between aging and disabilities that we have not focused upon, such as housing and other environmental adaptations for persons with disabilities, the intricacies of public or private disability insurance for rehabilitation and independent living services, and the need to forge a process to decide "reasonable accommodation" in implementing the Americans with Disabilities Act and the Fair Housing Act. Finally, the recession of the American economy and the deficits in the budgets of many states cannot be overlooked as possible deterrents to efforts in finding common ground between aging and disabilities and pursuing a unified agenda.

The adage that "all politics is ultimately local" applies to the exploration of common ground between the aging and disabilities systems. If change is to be made, if resources are to be shared, if the rehabilitation, aging, and developmental disabilities communities are to learn from each other, let the process begin locally. We need not wait for national initiatives. Convene local planning committees. Explore local needs and resources. We hope that this special volume helps in the process.

REFERENCES

Ansello, E. F., 1988. "The Intersecting of Aging and Disabilities." *Educational Gerontology* 14(5):351-64.

Ansello, E. F. and Rose, T., 1989. *Aging and Lifelong Disabilities: Partnership for the Twenty-First Century.* Palm Springs, Calif.: Elvirita Lewis Foundation.

Brody, S. J. and Ruff, G. E., 1986. *Aging and Rehabilitation: Advances in the State of the Art.* New York: Springer.

Brody, S. J. and Pawlson, L. G., 1990. *Aging and Rehabilitation II: The State of the Practice.* New York: Springer.

Council on Aging/Developmental Disabilities of Greater New York, 1990. *Glossary of Terms, Concepts, and Resources in the Fields of Aging and Developmental Disabilities.* New York: Brookdale Center on Aging.

Institute of Medicine, Committee on a National Research Agenda on Aging, 1991. *Extending Life, Enhancing Life: A National Research Agenda on Aging,* E. T. Lonergan, ed. Washington, D.C.: National Academy of Sciences.

Janicki, M. P., 1991. *Building the Future: Planning and Community Development in Aging and Developmental Disabilities.* Albany: New York State Office of Mental Retardation and Developmental Disabilities.

Janicki, M. P. and Wisniewski, H. M., eds., 1985. *Aging and Developmental Disabilities: Issues and Approaches.* Baltimore, Md.: Brookes.

LaPlante, M., 1989. "Disability in Basic Life Activities Across the Life Span." *Disability Statistics Report, No. 1.* San Francisco: Institute for Health and Aging, University of California.

Mahoney, C., Estes, C. and Heumann, J. E., 1986. *Toward a Unified Agenda: Proceedings of a National Conference on Disability and Aging.* San Francisco: Institute for Health and Aging, University of California, and Berkeley, Calif.: World Institute on Disability.

Pawlson, L. G. and Brody, S. J., 1991. *Rehabilitation and Geriatric Education: Perspectives and Potential.* Richmond, Va.: The Circle, Inc.

Ries, P. and Brown, S., 1991. Disability and Health: "Characteristics of Persons by Limitation of Activity and Assessed Health Status, United States, 1984-88." *Advance Data from Vital and Health Statistics* no. 197. Hyattsville, Md.: National Center for Health Statistics.

Rose, T. and Ansello, E. F., 1987. *Aging and Developmental Disabilities: Research and Planning* (Final Report to the Maryland State Planning Council on Developmental Disabilities). College Park: The University of Maryland Center on Aging.

Simon-Rusinowitz, L., 1991. "Toward a Unified Long-Term Care Agenda: Efforts Past and Present." Presentation at the 44th Annual Scientific Meeting of the Gerontological Society of America, San Francisco, Calif., Nov.

Chapter 2

Seeking Common Ground Between Aging and Developmental Disabilities

Edward F. Ansello

The gift of time has been broadly distributed. Increases in longevity have affected not only "mainstream" Americans, but also those with formerly life-stunting disabilities like mental retardation and cerebral palsy, enabling a true old age for the first time in history. At the same time, these very increases in life expectancy have allowed late-onset disabilities like Alzheimer's disease and blindness to become more common among elders after lifetimes of nondisabled adulthood. As Minkler (1990) notes, whatever the outcome of the controversy between the pandemic theory of disability (LaPlante, 1989), which correlates future increases in disability with increases in longevity, and the compression of morbidity hypothesis (Fries, 1984), which predicts decreases in disability, the reality today is that there are already more elders than ever before with either lifelong developmental disabilities or late-onset disabilities, or both. We have given some details on these numbers elsewhere (Ansello, 1988; Ansello and Eustis, 1992).

Disabilities and aging, actively dissociated by gerontologists and aging-related advocates for decades, are increasingly intersecting. Although age does not equal disability, disabilities are increasingly a factor in late life. While those at this intersection—researchers, educators, policy makers, and practitioners in both the aging and disabilities "systems"—have had no logical reason for past interaction, they now need to be aware of how the systems and their clientele may be entering common ground.

This chapter will focus on the broad aging network and the even broader disabilities system, concentrating on developmental disabilities. It will of necessity refer to each field as a "system," at times suggesting more cohesion than may in many instances apply. The purpose is analytical, not literal. This chapter will examine the emerging intersection in five steps by noting (1) factors in increased longevity of adults with developmental disabilities, (2) cross-cutting issues that traverse the supposed gaps between the two systems, (3) practical barriers to intersystem cooperation, (4) suggested means of overcoming these impediments, and (5) prospective agendas to help ensure that the systems operate to benefit the elder, whatever his or her characteristics.

FACTORS IN INCREASED LONGEVITY OF ADULTS WITH LIFELONG DISABILITIES

The causes of changes in human life expectancy are always multiple, complex, and interrelated. Certainly two of the more significant contributors to the aging of adults with lifelong developmental disabilities are improved healthcare and lengthened survival of parents. Advances in healthcare are of signal importance because improvements in treating such conditions as diabetes, hypertension, obesity, and cardiovascular diseases have meant that persons with lifelong impairments are better able to survive what were for them life-stunting diseases. Pharmacotherapeutical agents like beta blockers, for example, have made breakthroughs in treating hypertension, angina, and irregular heartbeat. As a result, adults with developmental disabilities are more apt to live through the threats that would have been fatal in the past.

The increased longevity of parents has relevance because the majority of all persons with developmental disabilities live in the community with their families. For example, Seltzer et al. (1991) note that across all ages fewer than 20 percent of those with mental retardation live in a licensed residential setting. Rose and Ansello (1987) estimate that some 60 percent of older adults with developmental disabilities in Maryland not only live with their families in the community, but also do so without formal services from any disabilities, aging, or social service agency. Indeed, in as yet unpublished research the Rappahannock-Rapidan Community Services Board in Virginia reports that the most successful way of *discovering* adults with developmental disabilities (84 families with a member who has developmental disabilities, including 20 elders, in the past year) has been through personal contacts, that is, relatives and friends who tell senior advocates associated with the agency of the existence of the family.

Another common mode of discovery is what Stokesberry (1989) calls the "four o'clock on a Friday afternoon syndrome," the telephone call from a relative saying that Aunt Mae has just died leaving cousin Sonny, who has had a lifelong impairment, in need of help—when until that moment no one in the agency had known of their existence. Clearly, since aging with developmental disabilities so often involves a community setting of private informal caregiving or assistance by parents, a lengthened life expectancy for the parents means that their offspring enjoy added years of the care and support that contribute to their own longevity.

CROSS-CUTTING ISSUES

In the past, little reason has existed for meaningful systematic interaction between the aging and disabilities systems. The developmental disabilities system has been focused historically on the client's first years of life in the assumption that early intervention would produce the greatest benefits; moreover, few clients survived to old age. The broad aging network has been funded since its inception with the amendments to the Older Americans Act of 1965 to concentrate on large numbers of elders; hence, a senior center may be staffed with one paid employee to 300–400 members. Nonetheless, there are strikingly similar chords in the music that the two systems dance to. Awareness of the similarities between the systems might help to lessen the perception of overwhelming differences and might advance recognition of some common ground. "Cross-cutting issues" (Ansello and Rose, 1989) include the following.

Marginality of Clientele

Both systems face some degree of bias against their clients. Though arguably less so today, elders have historically been disenfranchised socially because of retirement and old age. Disenfranchisement is also true for persons with disabilities. Both elders and those with disabilities have faced some form of segregation into specialized housing. Pointedly, Cohen (1988) argues that ageism today is focused upon those who combine the characteristics of age and disability. He calls this bias the "elderly mystique."

Family Caregiving

For those in both systems who need and want assistance, family caregiving has been a mainstay. In both the aging and disabilities systems, family caregiving reflects the simultaneous realities of (1) community, not institutional, living being the norm; (2) chronic care occurring in "convoys" of family and friendship networks, e.g., through siblings' involvement (Seltzer et al., 1991); and (3) underrecognized reliance upon and insufficient assistance to caregivers in the family. Cohen (1992), Eustis and Fischer (1992), Racino and Heumann (1992) and others, of course, argue persuasively for further incorporation of the independent living movement's emphasis upon autonomy and client-directed (and paid) personal assistance. Historically, however, one should see the common debt that both systems owe to family caregiving.

Contributions by Clients

Both systems labor under a generalized lack of appreciation for the roles their clients can play as "agents." Aging and disabilities advocates often place greater emphasis upon protecting and caring for their clients than upon charging or empowering them to action. At some point, continuous advocacy for services and resources to one's clients may raise perceptions of a "drain" being caused by them and questions of equity. This is much more likely to happen on the aging side of the comparison but does not diminish the point that many clients in both systems are individuals who can give something to others. I think of the man with Down's syndrome I saw at an adult daycare center in Maryland carefully helping an elder with Alzheimer's disease to eat his lunch.

Heterogeneity

The clients in both the aging and disabilities systems are heterogeneous. This means that within their group they grow more diverse and less alike with age. Accordingly, group work and categorical programming is less appropriate, not more, as clients age. Personnel in both systems are being challenged to respond meaningfully with individualized opportunities.

Goal Clarity

It seems fair to say that the goals of neither system are unequivocably clear or universally accepted. This has basic but as yet underplayed implications for those attempting to advance a "unified agenda" between the systems. For instance, what are the purposes of aging services?—to buttress self-sufficiency, to serve those in greatest need, to help one to grow and to become? Why do senior centers exist?—to serve as a community focal point, a safety net for health and nutrition, a place for social and recreational activities, or a membership organization? If the senior center's purpose can be and has been any one of the above, how can one globally advocate the integration of senior centers by elders with mental retardation without reference to the specific elders and centers in question?

PRACTICAL BARRIERS TO INTERSYSTEM COOPERATION

In seeking common ground, there is no shortage in the number of impediments to cooperation. At least nine have practical significance.

Unfamiliar Language, Philosophy, and Priorities in the Complementary System

Not only are terms and priorities different between the two systems (e.g., active treatment, generic services, entitlements) but also, to paraphrase George Bernard Shaw, aging and disabilities are separated by a common language: day programs in disabilities and daycare in aging are very different phenomena. Even within the disabilities system, differences in meaning obtain: Independent living programs in the field of blindness refer to skills training and counseling, whereas the independent living movement of disability advocates emphasizes empowerment, rights, and community organization as well.

Problematic Numbers and Dissociation Within Developmental Disabilities

The total number of older Americans with developmental disabilities is subject to debate, for several reasons. First, being primarily community dwellers and not institutional residents, and receiving no formal services or programs, they are not figured in agency "counts." Second, and perhaps more important, number estimates are complicated by disagreements on who is under or wants to be under the DD umbrella. Because the Developmental Disabilities Assistance and Bill of Rights Act grew from an emphasis upon brain dysfunction (i.e., only mental retardation, autism, epilepsy, and cerebral palsy were in the first act), some networks have distanced themselves, even though their clients qualify as satisfying the legal definition of a developmental disability. Consequently, there is little of what might be considered intrasystem cooperation, let alone networking, within the loose disabilities field. So, organizations for the blind, for example, may not consider themselves part of the DD system, and may not typically share numbers, data, or resources. Even organizations for persons with cerebral palsy (CP), aware that the vast majority of persons with CP do not have mental retardation, tend not to network with the developmental disabilities system which, by default and by virtue of the large core of its clients and professionals, has been dominated by those concerned with mental retardation. The acronym for the system is often expressed as MR/DD, reflecting at once the dominance of the field of mental retardation and the simultaneous connection and disconnection between it and other developmental disabilities.

Differences in Funding Streams and Operations Between the Systems

With developmental disabilities services—for example, those in mental retardation—money essentially follows the clients; participating clients have individualized service programs that carry funding for a range of activities, which may change as needs change. The aging system is more an organizationally oriented hierarchy, with funding formulas that trickle down to agencies on the basis of gross numbers of elders in a geographic area. Being more individually oriented, disabilities services commonly have waiting lists for slots in day treatment programs and in vocational rehabilitation. Maryland's Developmental Disabilities Administration has over 5,000 names on its "Band A" of qualified clients who are awaiting openings or slots for services.

Further, more than in the aging system, for-profit operators have a significant presence in some states' disabilities services. Gettings (1988) notes that there are several models of operation for state mental retardation programs, compared to the one prevailing aging network mode.

Lack of Clear-Cut Goals

As mentioned above, there are varying opinions about the purpose of aging services. The DD system is driven in large measure by a vocational rehabilitation agenda. As Janicki (1991), Raia (1992), Sutton et al. (1992) and others have asked in essence, what happens to a money- follows-the-client system when clients become too old to justify their continued training, when they "age out" of the system's reason for being?

Unlikelihood of a Unified Agenda

How much inhibitory pressure does the expectation of a unitary or unified agenda for the two systems exert on personnel within each system, especially when they are already wrestling with goals and philosophies being called into question by the increasing special needs of elders and the increasing aging of adults with disabilities? Is the goal of a unified agenda perceived as a burden, stymying initial action by anyone other than visionaries?

Differences in Perceived Benefits from Cooperation

Questions arise as to who would benefit if the aging and disabilities systems were integrated. I have heard senior center directors ask, "What do we get out of this? How does my center benefit by integrating three or four elders with developmental disabilities?" Up to this point, the practical focus of the discussion by professionals at the intersection has been largely on integrating clients with developmental disabilities into the aging system, with much less attention to the benefits the aging system might derive from the disabilities system, say, from sharing resources and skills used in mental retardation and developmental disabilities to assist elders with Alzheimer's disease.

Lack of a Nonthreatening Broker

The aura of an arranged marriage orchestrated by others may have a chilling effect upon cross-system research, education, policy development, and service. We have found that a relatively neutral third party, in our instance an institution of higher education, can play the part of a nonthreatening "marriage broker" in bringing together personnel from the two systems to address their common needs and resources.

Trees Versus Forest Mentality (or Crisis Management)

Workers in human services often labor in a crisis management atmosphere; in dealing with seemingly endless budget cuts and demands for serving yet another qualified group, the tendency is to hunker down to protect one's own. We hear about "my clients" and "my services." Those not previously in one's system are thought of as outsiders. We call this mind-set "mental geography."

Shortage of Cross-Trained Personnel

In negotiating the coming together of two systems, even if only to explore resource sharing, experts in the background and operations of both systems are needed. Between disabilities and aging, the knowledge gap, of course, is considerable. Within the broad disabilities system itself, however, the dissociation mentioned previously has led to insularity, so that professionals in the field of hearing impairment know little about the field of cerebral palsy, those in mental retardation know little about visual impairment, and so forth. The current shortage of such cross-trained people may be the most critical barrier to finding common ground. Their presence would facilitate the confronting of such intermediate barriers as differences in language, regulations, and perceived benefits.

SUGGESTED MEANS OF OVERCOMING IMPEDIMENTS

Our experiences with the Partners Project in Maryland, 1987–90, and Partners II in Virginia, 1990–92, demonstrate that barriers to cooperation between the systems, if not integration, can be overcome by actions of a committed third party cooperating with members of both systems (Ansello and Zink, 1990; Ansello et al., 1991). In brief, the lessons of the Partners Projects are that cross-training programs based on local needs; mechanisms for exposure to the complementary system, like site visits; and exchange of personnel through internships or cooperative agreements are all keynotes to redressing the shortage of cross-trained personnel, a principal barrier to intersystem cooperation. Fundamentally, the projects are effective in developing local resources that remain after the expiration of the grant, such as joint planning committees and local experts in aging and developmental disabilities who can respond to continuing needs.

The Partners Project in Maryland was a collaboration of the University of Maryland Center on Aging, the Maryland State Office on Aging, and the Maryland Developmental Disabilities Administration. Supported by the Administration on Aging, it addressed several levels of this new intersection of aging and developmental disabilities, including the need for understanding the clientele, priorities, funding streams, language, and mechanics of the complementary system; identifying resources that can be used effectively in serving clients at this intersection; confronting policy and attitudinal barriers against retardation and other disabilities; planning for the interaction of the systems in order to capitalize on each other's expertise in aging and in disabilities; and acting to integrate clientele and resources.

The several team members of the Partners Project initiated a developmental series of activities designed to address local needs in a manner that would have enduring impact on intersystem cooperation. First, the project convened a Statewide Advisory Council whose membership includes directors of public and private agencies and organizations in aging and in the several developmental disabilities. The council proved to be a microcosm of aging and developmental disabilities in Maryland, fractionated and initially protective of "turf," but ultimately strongly supportive. Some of these council members subsequently participated in each activity of the project. Second, the project convened Regional Planning Committees, one in each of four geographic areas of the state, comprised of program directors, policy analysts, planners, managers, and service providers from the two systems as well as representatives from "consumer" constituencies (elders and adults with developmental disabilities) and from such allied fields as adult protective services and health departments. The council and the Regional Planning Committee determined statewide and local priorities, respectively, for "cross-training," i.e., topical on-site education targeted to the characteristics of the older adults in each region and taught in a manner suitable to the characteristics of the personnel in the two systems. The Regional Committees suggested content, speakers, times, and locations.

Third, the needs-oriented training sessions brought personnel from both systems together at an aging or a DD agency site that served as host for plenary and concurrent sessions. Local and project staff members served as trainers, in order to develop local expertise even among individuals without prior experience as trainers. The project conducted over 80 such training sessions across the state, attended by over 600 professionals and paraprofessionals. Session topics ranged from introductory to advanced and were designated in advance as appropriate for persons in either the aging or developmenal disabilities fields, or both. Topics included Aging and Developmental Disabilities; Transitions in the Lives of People with Developmental Disabilities; Client Assessment; Drugs and the Elderly: High Use/High Risk Medications; Addressing Social/Sexual Behavior of Adults with Developmental Disabilities; Effective Use of Community Resources; Helping Adults with Mental Retardation in Confronting Death; Integrating Adults with MR/DD into Senior Centers, etc. Participants took pre- and post-tests on content. Each training day's content, in turn, was assessed by means of participants' gain scores and evaluations of the sessions.

Fourth, the project enabled interested participants to experience other forms of learning in addition to the local cross-training sessions. It presented workshops at the state conferences of aging agencies in 1988, 1989, and 1990. The project's core staff has taught an academic course, "Aging and Disabilities," at the Institute for Gerontological Practice at the University of Maryland, College Park, since the summer of 1989. The project director developed and coedited a special issue of a professional journal that was devoted to aging and disabilities, *Educational Gerontology* 14(5), 1988, making the issue broadly available for individual scholarship. And the project team convened two large-scale conferences on aging and disabilities, both lifelong and late-onset, one in College Park in May 1989, which was statewide, and the other in Philadelphia in January 1990, which was multistate. Overall, these allowed individuals several opportunities to become more knowledgeable at very limited expense and proved, in practice, to be effective means of developing cross-trained expertise in each of the state's four regions.

The Partners Project also brokered short-term "internship" or exchange experiences in which professionals from one system were placed in the complementary system at a parallel organization and professional level; some 22 individuals undertook these mini-internships of one to three days, gaining valuable insights and personal acquaintances.

Finally, the project team has developed *The Partners Project Handbook*, a training manual for in-service education in aging and developmental disabilities. The manual is composed of 13 self-contained modules that can be taught by agency staff; each reflects the most effective training content, as determined by comparing participants' pre- and post-cognitive gains and evaluations. The Partners Project used its own staff and commissioned local people who served as the local trainers to write modules 10–15 pages in length, each of which is preceded by a statement of objectives and followed by suggested readings and audiovisual supplements. Manual contents include "Practical Aspects of Program Implementation," "Programming for Older Developmentally Disabled Persons with Adult Onset Handicaps," and "Contributions by Elders with Developmental Disabilities."

Partners II is the informal name of an AoA-funded project in Virginia entitled "Improving Services to Older Persons with Developmental Disabilities—Policy, Training, and Service," which builds upon the successes of the 1987–90 Partners Project in Maryland and a recent (1989–90) collaboration between aging and developmental disabilities agencies in Virginia (Wood, 1991). Partners II involves the Virginia Department for the Aging; the Board for Rights of Virginians with Disabilities; two units at Virginia Commonwealth University, namely the Virginia Center on Aging and the Virginia Institute for Developmental Disabilities; the Virginia Department of Mental Health, Mental Retardation, and Substance Abuse Services; and three local agencies—the Rappahannock-Rapidan Community Services Center, the Norfolk Senior Center, and the SEVAMP Area Agency on Aging.

Partners II staff are analyzing the status of, and barriers to, coordination and integration of aging and DD service systems in Virginia through a series of in-person interviews and mailed questionnaires with different levels of personnel in a broad range of aging and disabilities-related agencies, from autism to head injury. These are some of the questions being asked: How does an agency determine the clientele it serves? How does it identify, if at all, older persons with developmental disabilities and their needs? How does it appropriate human and material resources and what are its service objectives? Partners II project staff are also capitalizing upon extant Regional Planning Committees (RPCs) that were established in the earlier Virginia collaboration. These RPCs are identifying prioritized local needs and local expertise for cross-training content. Cognitive gains by participants and their evaluations of cross-training sessions have been very positive. RPCs are also supplying administrators and service providers for a project-brokered internship exchange between the systems. Further,

Partners II staff are helping the Norfolk Senior Center, an urban agency, and the Rappahannock-Rapidan Community Services Board, a rural agency, to identify both federal and parallel nonfederal resources that can be made available to elders and caregivers of elders with developmental disabilities in order to assist them to remain relatively independent in the community.

PROSPECTIVE AGENDAS TO HELP ENSURE THAT SYSTEMS BENEFIT ELDERS

Having noted the demographic impetus for the aging and disabilities systems to interact, and having reviewed commonalities, barriers, and representative barrier busters, it is appropriate to step back and ask what is the obligation of government and others who profess the public good to those who age and have disabilities? Further, what needs to be done to satisfy this obligation?

The federal government may yet initiate a national program of entitlement for long-term care. Beedon (1992), Binstock (1992), DeJong et al. (1992), and Racino and Heumann (1992) among others have cogently assessed its merits and prospects. But if the federal government is not going to have an active role in chronic care, and if state and local governments are unable to do so because of "cost shifting" (Gettings, 1988; Medical Benefits, 1992) to them from the federal government, then at least these parties should ensure the continuance of long-term care by brokering or fostering more effective relationships between and among those most immediately involved in long-term care: clients, informal providers, and formal providers.

Federal, state, and local governments can advance the latter goal by relatively painless steps, including regulatory restructuring and support for targeted research and training initiatives. We suggest *regulatory restructuring* in three areas:

1. Greater allocations of resources for accessible and acceptable community-based care. Whereas most elders and most adults with disabilities live in a community context, most dollars go to institutional care. Medicaid waivers for community-based care should be broadened (Wallace, 1990).
2. Greater emphasis upon client-choice or client-centered programs of assistance. In many cases the client is able not only to control aspects of his or her assistance, but also to contribute to the functioning of the system itself. The Cooperative Caring

Network in Washington, D.C., is a recent start-up example of the concept of service credit brokering, long encouraged by the Robert Wood Johnson Foundation (Meiners et al., 1992), whereby the capabilities of individuals are tapped to assist peers with disabilities, and the contributing peer's services are credited by a brokering agency against future need.

3. More-substantial mechanisms to encourage real collaborations between and within aging and disabilities systems. Memoranda of agreement need to be *activated* to stimulate collaborative research, policy analyses, staff cross-training, internship exchanges, and problem solving so that funding channels are not allowed to create competition among groups that need similar kinds of assistance, pitting those who are elderly, or who have mental retardation, or head injuries, or visual impairments, or chronic mental illness against each other for a constantly shrinking piece of the pie. One of the finest accomplishments of the 1987 Wingspread Conference on Aging and Lifelong Disabilities (Ansello and Rose, 1989) was the supportive joint testimony subsequently given by two state aging and state disabilities directors before the appropriations committee of their state legislature. Each had participated fully in this Wingspread Conference.

Support for targeted research and training could add the knowledge necessary for everything from cooperative policy formulation to joint ventures in resource development. Areas of mutual interest for research and training include the following:

1. Investigation of a common etiology of Alzheimer's disease and Down's syndrome. Such a discovery would have enormous implications for prevention and treatment.
2. Identification of the many invisible community-dwelling survivors of lifelong developmental disabilities, of their extant resources for independent living, and precritically, of their anticipated needs for healthcare and for psychosocial and economic assistance.
3. Testing various means of formalizing and "informalizing" relationships between clients and providers in the two systems, between personnel in the two systems, and between the formal caregivers and informal caregivers (Seltzer et al., 1987). Formal (paid and licensed) providers and informal (unpaid family and friends) very seldom *inform* each other; indeed, there is an almost total lack of any systematic means for this to occur. To this point,

the new Vermont Department of Aging and Disabilities has asked the state's area agencies on aging to convene "provider-consumer consortia" in each of the five regions of the state with the goal of developing a community-assisted independent living system (Charron, 1992).

4. Research into the long-term impact of integrating systems and elders. What consequences might integration have upon the functioning of the two systems (e.g., cost savings, fund transfers); the functioning of elders with developmental disabilities (e.g., ability to retire from active treatment plans); the functioning of mainstream elders (e.g., altered perceptions of aging itself); the so-called feminization of aging (e.g., in some disabilities systems older males outnumber older females); and higher education curricula (e.g., lip-service given to cross- and multi-disciplinary education—which evaporates in budget-tightening).

The simultaneous increase in the numbers of adults with lifelong impairments and adults with late-onset disabilities is drawing two fairly different human-service systems toward a point of intersection. It is in the best interests of our clients and ourselves to explore the common ground before us.

REFERENCES

Ansello, E. F., 1988. "The Intersecting of Aging and Disabilities." *Educational Gerontology* 14(5): 351–64.

Ansello, E. F. and Rose, T., 1989. *Aging and Lifelong Disabilities: Partnership for the Twenty-First Century*. Palm Springs, Calif.: Elvirita Lewis Foundation.

Ansello, E. F. and Zink, M. B., 1990. "The Partners Project: Targetting Community-Based Research and Education on Aging and Developmental Disabilities." In W. R. Rivera and N. W. Clarke, eds., *Proceedings of the 1990 Lifelong Learning Research Conference*. Fairfax, Va.: George Mason University, pp. 118–24.

Ansello, E. F. and Eustis, N. N., 1992. "A Common Stake?" *Generations* 16(1):5 (herein, Chapter 1, p. 1).

Ansello, E. F. et al., 1991. "Partners II: Policy, Training, and Resources in Aging and Developmental Disabilities in Virginia." Paper presented at the 44th Annual Scientific Meeting of the Gerontological Society of America, San Francisco.

Beedon, L., 1992. "Autonomy as a Policy Goal for Disability and Aging." *Generations* 16(1):79 (herein, Chapter 18, p. 157).

Binstock, R. H., 1992. "Aging, Disability, and Long-Term Care: The Politics of Common Ground." *Generations* 16(1):83 (herein, Chapter 19, p. 165).

Charron, K., 1992. "Changing Complex Long-Term-Care Systems." *Generations* 16(1):97 (herein, Chapter 21, p. 193).

Cohen, E. S., 1988. "The Elderly Mystique: Constraints on the Autonomy of the Elderly with Disabilities." *Gerontologist* 28(1):24–31.

Cohen, E. S., 1992. "What Is Independence?" *Generations* 16(1):49 (herein Chapter 10, p. 91).

DeJong, G., Batavia, A. I. and McKnew, L. B., 1992. "The Independent Living Model of Personal Assistance in National Long-Term-Care Policy." *Generations* 16(1):89.

Eustis, N. N. and Fischer, L. R., 1992. "Common Needs, Different Solutions? Younger and Older Homecare Clients." *Generations* 16(1):17 (herein Chapter 3, p. 25).

Fries, J. F., 1984. "The Compression of Morbidity: Miscellaneous Comments about a Theme." *Gerontologist* 24(4): 354–59.

Gettings, R. M., 1988. "Barriers To and Opportunities For Cooperation between the Aging and Developmental Disabilities Service Delivery Systems." *Educational Gerontology* 14(5):419–29.

Janicki, M. P., 1991. *Building the Future: Planning and Community Development in Aging and Developmental Disabilities.* Albany: New York State Office of Mental Retardation and Developmental Disabilities.

LaPlante, M., 1989. "Disability in Basic Life Activities across the Life Span." *Disability Statistics Report,* No. 1. San Francisco: Institute for Health and Aging, University of California.

Medical Benefits, 1992. "Cost Shifting: When Benefit Payments Become Tax Payments." *Medical Benefits* 9(3):1.

Meiners, M. R., McKay, H. L. and Helfand, L., 1992. *National Directory of Service Credit Banking Programs.* College Park: University of Maryland Center on Aging.

Minkler, M., 1990. "Aging and Disability: Behind and Beyond the Stereotypes." *Journal of Aging Studies* 4(3): 245–60.

Racino, J. A. and Heumann, J. E., 1992. "Independent Living and Community Life: Building Coalitions Among Elders, People with Disabilities, and Our Allies." *Generations* 16(1):43 (herein Chapter 9, p. 79).

Raia, P. A., 1992. "What Are We Trying to Restore? A Case for Habilitation." *Generations* 16(1):37 (herein, Chapter 7, p. 69).

Rose T. and Ansello, E. F., 1987. *Aging and Developmental Disabilities: Research and Planning* (Final Report to the Maryland State Planning Council on Developmental Disabilities). College Park: The University of Maryland Center on Aging.

Seltzer, M. M., Ivry, J. and Litchfield, L. C., 1987. "Family Members as Case Managers: Partnership between the Formal and Informal Support Networks." *Gerontologist* 27(6): 722–28.

Seltzer, G. B. et al., 1991. "Adults with Mental Retardation and Their Aging Mothers: Impacts of Siblings." *Family Relations* 40: 310–17.

Stokesberry, J. L., 1989. "Best Practice for Integrating Service Delivery to Older Persons with Developmental Disabilities." In E. F. Ansello and T. Rose, eds., *Aging and Lifelong Disabilities: Partnership for the Twenty-First Century*. Palm Springs, Calif.: Elvirita Lewis Foundation.

Sutton, E., Sterns, H. L. and Roberts, R. S., 1992. "'Retirement' for Older Persons with Developmental Disabilities." *Generations* 16(1):63 (herein, Chapter 14, p. 121).

Wallace, S. B., 1990. "The No-Care Zone: Availability, Accessibility, and Acceptability in Community-Based Long-Term Care." *Gerontologist* 30(2): 254–61.

Wood, J. B., 1991. *The Aged and Aging Developmentally Disabled in Virginia: Project Report*. Richmond: Virginia Department for the Aging and Virginia Institute for Developmental Disabilities.

Chapter 3

Common Needs, Different Solutions? Younger and Older Homecare Clients

Nancy N. Eustis and Lucy Rose Fischer

To borrow from Shakespeare, some of us are born disabled, some achieve disability in old age, and some have disability thrust upon them at an age in between (R. L. Kane, 1991). Whatever the timing of onset, persons with physical disabilities often require assistance to function in daily activities. Further, no matter how long they have been disabled, most persons prefer to live at home or in a homelike setting rather than in a nursing home, chronic-care hospital, or other institution. Beyond a shared preference for staying out of nursing homes, however, the independent living movement of younger adults with disabilities, on the one hand, and people in the field of aging, on the other, have conceptualized and implemented the idea of living in the community very differently. This chapter discusses four areas of difference between the disability and aging communities with regard to independent living and illustrates these differences with findings from an exploratory study of 54 disabled persons, ranging in age from 27 to 99, and their paid helpers (who included home health aides, homemakers, and personal care attendants).

DIFFERING SERVICE STRATEGIES

As discussed by other authors in this volume, in the 1960s and 1970s young adults with developmental disabilities, traumatic injuries, and chronic or disabling illnesses organized to advocate for supportive services and other adaptations that would allow them to live in the community outside of an institution or their parental family (DeJong et al., 1992; Kailes, 1992; Racino and Heumann, 1992). The independent living movement emphasized empowerment of persons with disabilities (through such means as management of their own personal care assistants) and established independent living centers to involve and assist adults with disabilities. (See Budde, 1990 for a description of the independent living movement.) Parallel efforts in the 1970s and 1980s encouraged the provision of community-based or noninstitutional services for the elderly, including in-home services such as home healthcare, personal care, and homemaking as well as adult daycare for functionally impaired older persons (Eustis et al., 1984; Kane and Kane, 1987; Justice, 1988). These programs tend to emphasize case management to coordinate services, reduction of expenditures for nursing home care, and public regulation of providers to assure quality of care. A common element of independent living programs for both younger and older adults with disabilities is reliance on personal assistance services, such as those funded by Medicaid home- and community-based services waivers (Litvak et al., 1987; Litvak and Kennedy, 1991).

Since 1985 younger and older persons with disabilities and their advocates have discussed similarities and differences between the field of aging and the independent living movement (Mahoney, 1986; Simon-Rusinowitz and Hofland, pending). These discussions suggest differences concerning (1) the extent of reliance on unpaid caregivers, (2) the site of and rationale for providing care, (3) the extent of involvement of medical personnel in care arrangements and provision, and (4) the extent to which the disabled person directs and manages his or her services and assistants.

COMPARING OLDER AND YOUNGER HOMECARE USERS

The authors contacted homecare agencies in metropolitan Minneapolis and more rural southeastern Minnesota and obtained names of younger (under 65) and older (65-plus) clients who regularly received two or more visits per week and would need (or had received) homecare for at least six months. Agencies also provided the name of the worker serving each client. We obtained the names of those clients who hire their own aides from help-wanted ads and by word of mouth. The clients we interviewed included 20 younger adults under 65, and 34 adults age 65 and older. These clients included 22 persons, 10 of whom were over age 60, who had been disabled by developmental disabilities or early-onset chronic conditions such as cerebral palsy and multiple sclerosis. We conducted one- to two-hour semistructured interviews with each client and (except in two cases) with the client's worker. (For a more complete report on the research, see Eustis and Fischer, 1991, and Fischer and Eustis, in press.)

The subsamples of younger and older clients were similar in several important ways. On average, each subsample reported help (paid or unpaid) with seven activities of daily living (ADLs) and instrumental activities of daily living (IADLs), and the majority of each subsample reported being disabled for two or more years. Forty percent of each subsample lived alone, and 80 percent of each group would have needed to be in a nursing home without paid help, according to interviewer judgments. However, there were also important differences: The older clients had more medical problems; more of the younger clients could not walk; and the younger clients received more hours of care. We discuss these and other comparisons below. It is important to note that the sample is small, nonrandom, and probably biased toward "good" agency clients and "good" agency-employed workers (because they were suggested by participating agencies).

1. *Reliance on unpaid caregivers*. Having assistants who are paid has been a hallmark of the independent living movement. Proponents oppose relying on informal or unpaid help because the care receiver has no clout over a volunteer caregiver, the means for holding the unpaid caregiver accountable are limited, and unpaid caregivers may be burdened (Batavia et al., 1991; Heumann, 1991; DeJong et al., 1992; Racino and Heumann, 1992). In particular, for persons who are disabled at a young age, moving out of the parental home has been an important part of being independent.

In contrast, most of the community-dwelling elderly who get assistance with activities of daily living receive help from family members and other unpaid caregivers. In a recent national survey, of the 4.65 million persons in the community with a chronic disability, 90 percent reported family help, and 25 percent reported getting in-home services rendered by a paid attendant (Hanley et al., 1991). Gerontologists have two different hypotheses about preferences of the elderly for paid versus family help (Chappell, 1990). The "substitution hypothesis" states that older persons prefer family help to paid help—specifically that they prefer, in rank order, help from a spouse, from an adult child (usually a daughter), from a sibling, and only as a last choice, from a paid helper. A second hypothesis is that there is a complementary relationship between paid and unpaid help (see Litwak, 1985). For example, there is evidence that the very old prefer assistance from persons who are paid and not part of their immediate social support network (Antonucci, 1990), although this may be due to their having fewer family members available (see, for example, Fischer et al., 1989). Further, at least one study has shown that elderly persons prefer to receive personal care and housekeeping help from persons who are paid (Brody et al., as reported by Chappell, 1990).

In the authors' Minnesota study, the older homecare clients had more family available because they were more likely to be married, to have children, and to live with a spouse or other relative. The older subsample reported getting, on average, more help on ADL and IADL tasks from family and friends than did the younger homecare clients. Older clients were also more likely to say that a family member had made or participated in the decision about homecare. Almost a third of the elderly homecare clients lived with a spouse or an adult child who was a primary caregiver or care manager.

While over half of the older clients lived with family, this was true for only one-quarter of the younger clients. And in only one instance was a spouse a primary caregiver for a younger client. However, those younger clients living with a spouse or children did rely on them for some assistance. For example, a young man with quadriplegia due to a spinal cord injury got help from his 6-year-old son in many ways, such as opening jars or cans while preparing meals. A 50-year-old woman with cerebral palsy lived with her mother who was over 80; the mother did all the arranging for help, and both got assistance in dressing from the morning aide. Both younger and older clients called on their families in case of an emergency or received supplementary help such as transportation or yard work.

2. *Involvement of medical professionals* in arrangements for in-home services is regarded as intrusive and unnecessary by the independent living movement (Heumann, 1986; DeJong and Wenker, 1987; Zola, 1988; Racino and Heumann, 1992; DeJong et al., 1992). Hence, younger adults with disabilities often prefer to hire their workers directly rather than use agency-provided in-home services, because public regulations as well as agency procedures usually require that a physician and nurse be involved in determining a care plan and in supervising services. In contrast, older persons more frequently use homecare agencies.

The Minnesota study demonstrated these differences. In this study, younger clients were more likely to hire their workers directly, while proportionately more older persons obtained agency services. More older clients indicated that a doctor or other professional made or was involved in the decision to get homecare. Further, workers who assisted the elderly clients were more likely to be employed full time, to be certified nursing assistants, and to think of homecare as a career than were workers for younger clients.

It is unclear whether these differences have to do with the health status of the client, the amount of care needed, the rules of public programs that pay for homecare, or client preference. More of the older clients had unstable medical conditions and reported being in pain, although the two subsamples were equally likely to report being in the hospital during the preceding year. Many of the younger clients got more paid help and may have found it cheaper to hire workers directly. Further, Minnesota's personal-care attendant program under Medicaid had allowed eligible adults under 65 to employ "independent providers."

Both younger and older respondents talked about the advantages of getting help from an agency versus getting help from workers hired directly. For younger clients whose care was paid for by Minnesota's Medicaid program, this issue was particularly salient because, at the time of our interviews, the state had just implemented a rule change requiring that personal care attendants be agency employees. One woman in her 20s said, "No way would I get a worker from an agency because I would lose control." Another younger client was firmly opposed to his attendant being required to keep records of the client's care and to periodic home visits by an agency nurse. Fortunately, this client and the agency were in the process of working out a compromise. One client said, "I wouldn't get help from an agency because they'll hire anyone who walks through the door." In contrast, several younger clients mentioned that now that they worked with an agency, they didn't need to scramble so much for backup care because the agency could provide a substitute worker if the regular person was unable to come.

Criticisms of agency workers by older clients included (1) workers' schedules being inflexible (so that a worker could not do anything extra like putting lotion on dry skin), (2) the agency switching workers and schedules without informing the client, and (3) inadequate screening and hiring practices. In contrast, one older women with cerebral palsy said she now felt "too vulnerable" to hire workers directly, although she had done so when she was younger. "You say something that hurts their feelings and they never come back."

3. *Location of care.* A third difference between the way services are provided in the field of aging and the preferences of the independent living movement has to do with whether assistance is provided to the client outside of his or her home (Simon-Rusinowitz and Hofland, pending). Younger persons with disabilities and their advocates argue that personal assistance should be provided in the community, not just in the home of the disabled person. In contrast, public programs that reimburse care for older persons seldom allow for assistance outside the residence except if an excursion has a medical purpose. This difference may originate in the rationale for providing care. For younger persons, rehabilitation and independent living services were originally justified when returning to work was a goal, so assistance at work and with getting to and from the workplace was a reimbursable expense. For older persons the rationale for services is keeping people out of institutions, hence the emphasis on care provided in one's residence. In addition, agency policies may prevent agency-employed in-home workers from assisting their clients outside the home.

Younger clients in the study sample were more likely to be working and to be participating in volunteer activities. Twice as many older as younger clients said they did not get out of the house most days. (Older clients who lived outside of the Twin Cities were especially likely to stay in their homes.) Some of the older clients reported needing assistance to get out. However, some younger clients also saw their worker as providing a way to get out. One younger client was worried about what he would do when his live-in attendant took another job; he didn't think he would find someone else who would enjoy the social activities he shared with the worker. A 50-year-old woman with cerebral palsy participated in church and other activities but often lacked the help she needed to attend in person.

4. *Client-managed in-home care.* Client control of service arrangements and personal assistants has been a fundamental precept of the independent living movement. This principle is an important reason for the movement's insistence that public funding of personal assistance services allow persons with disabilities to hire their own workers directly rather than require agency-provided services, because the client of an independent provider has the authority to select, select, train, supervise, pay and, if necessary, fire the worker (Litvak et al., 1987; DeJong and Wenker, 1987; WID, 1991; Batavia et al., 1991; Zola, 1988). A function of independent living centers, then, is providing skills

training, peer support, and information and referral to empower clients to manage their own care (Cole, 1987). Being in charge or autonomous also enhances the well-being of older persons with disabilities (see, for example, Hofland, 1990). Sabatino and Litvak (1992) identify four elements of client management of services.The client must (1) have a choice of service provider, (2) have a choice of services, (3) train the worker, and (4) supervise the worker.

Findings from the Minnesota study suggest an even broader understanding of *taking charge* of homecare arrangements and services, which includes the following: (1) getting information about homecare, (2) making or participating in the decision to use paid in-home help, (3) participating in developing the care plan or deciding on the worker's tasks, (4) training the worker, (5) supervising the worker, (6) giving the worker positive or negative feedback about her or his performance, (7) communicating with the homecare agency about needed services or worker performance, (8) arranging for a way to get help in case of an emergency or when the paid worker does not come as scheduled, and (9) being able to articulate attributes of a desirable homecare worker or agency.

Proportionately more younger clients reported making the decision about homecare, training and supervising the worker, and giving the worker positive or negative feedback about her or his performance. In addition, younger clients were more likely to hire their workers directly, as reported above. (See Table 1.)

Roughly one third of the older clients took charge in at least three of the above ten ways. These clients tended to be in their 60s and 70s (although one was over 80) and to have been disabled for many years. They tended to be without family (or without relatives who were involved in their care). A majority had developmental or early-onset disabilities such as cerebral palsy, polio, or multiple sclerosis. Two of these older clients mentioned experience with the independent living movement. For example, one woman who seemed to have a life-long cognitive impairment spoke proudly of knowing how to show the aide to give her eyedrops and of being taught to take her own medication. Some of the clients who appeared to be more passive about their care arrangements and helpers tended to be quite ill (or in a medically unstable condition) and were more likely than other clients in the sample to have cognitive or hearing impairments. A substantial portion of the more passive clients had family available who interacted with the worker or the agency and took charge. Other clients who were more passive received only help with

Table 1. Selected Ways in Which Clients 'Take Charge' of In-Home Services

	Number of Clients by Client Age (N = 54)		
Ways of Taking Charge	Up to Age 60 n = 21	Age 61-70 n = 8	Age 71-99 n = 25
Did you have enough information regarding homecare?			
Yes	16 (82)[a]	4 (50)[a]	11 (44)[a]
No	1 (19)	4 (50)	7 (28)
Who made the decision about homecare?			
Client	16 (86)	4 (50)	10 (40)
Family	1 (5)	2 (25)	7 (28)
M.D./social worker/other	2 (10)	2 (25)	8 (32)
Did you participate in the following:			
Training the worker?	17 (86)	3 (38)	7 (28)
Supervising the worker?	15 (71)	3 (38)	10 (40)
Giving direct praise to the worker?	14 (76)	5 (63)	11 (44)
Criticizing the worker directly?	13 (66)	2 (25)	6 (24)
Worker employed by:			
Homecare agency	7 (33)[b]	4 (75)	21 (84)[c]
Directly by client	13 (66)	1 (25)	4 (16)

[a]Percentage of those responding is in parentheses.
[b]Younger clients whose direct-hire workers were reimbursed by Medicaid.
[c]Several older clients hired helpers directly as well as using an agency-employed aide.

homemaking and, in some instances, weekly assistance with taking a bath. Perhaps, because they needed less help they had less stake in directing their care.

The Minnesota study also suggests another dimension to taking charge. The study showed that younger clients were proportionately more likely to think of the paid assistant as a "worker" or "worker and friend" while older clients were proportionately more likely to say their worker is a "friend" or "like family."

HOW RELEVANT TO ELDERS IS THE INDEPENDENT LIVING MOVEMENT?

How much common ground underlies the approaches of younger and older adults to getting their needs met? This is a question that merits ongoing debate and inquiry. Our data suggest some partial answers from the viewpoint of persons now using homecare (other studies of the perspectives of older and younger homecare clients include Reif, 1990; Management Group, 1990; Vivone and Kaplan, 1990; Kimmich, 1991). Older homecare clients in the Minnesota study relied somewhat more on family members, professionals, and homecare agencies than did younger clients, and proportionately more younger clients reported making the decision about homecare as well as training and supervising the worker. However, there was overlap in how the younger and older subsamples in the Minnesota study got their needs met. Younger and older clients used a variety of care arrangements, including paid in-home workers, family members and neighbors, as well as electronic devices such as Lifeline and pagers. They valued continuity, dependability, and flexibility in a worker and in their homecare arrangements. Clients of any age depended at times on workers as well as family members for emotional support and for activities. Clients of all ages, or in some cases family members, took charge of homecare arrangements.

Study findings do not allow us to determine the extent to which observed differences between the older and younger clients have to do with inherent features of the aging process or with other possible explanations. Observed differences between older and younger clients in care arrangements seemed to reflect differences in the clients' health status, the availability of family members, and regulations regarding the reimbursement of service providers, as well as differences in client age. When older clients who took charge were compared with older clients who did not, additional factors emerged. Clients who took charge tended to receive more hours of paid help and have more experience in dealing with paid help; most but not all were without impairments in communication or cognitive ability. Moreover, some of the differences between younger and older client that were observed in this study may not be true of future generations of homecare users; for example, increasing numbers of younger adults with AIDS will have long-term need for medical as well as personal-care services, and older women clients in the future may be more assertive as current advocates and a more informed generation of consumers grows older.

It is important to note that considerations of cost and quality assurance are often more important than client needs and preferences in determining homecare arrangements. For example, policies encourage family caregiving and prohibit provision of services outside the home in order to constrain costs and reduce liability of paid providers. Moreover, physicians and case managers often are involved in care arrangements so that they can certify that the client is eligible for (in need of) services and to guard against providing unnecessary (i.e., too costly) care. In addition, public and private insurers frequently prefer agency-provided care because the agency can be held responsible for screening and supervising the worker.

There are also system issues such as the separation or integration of acute and long-term-care services, which affect what services are available to and used by clients of varying ages. In one state that has a program of in-home services for both younger and older clients, older clients reportedly use services proportionately less than do younger clients, in part because the program was designed without linkages to hospitals and other healthcare providers (McDowell, 1991).

Responses of older clients in the Minnesota study indicated that many felt they needed more information about homecare. There was also evidence of clients having very little understanding of how homecare was arranged and supervised. On the other hand, several older clients told of getting help from the homecare agency or a case manager in deciding it was okay to request a different worker or find a different agency. These findings would suggest the relevance of training disabled older persons in such tasks as how to give the worker feedback about her or his performance. In fact, clients of all ages may need help in negotiating relationships with their workers. Another contribution of the independent living movement is involvement of persons with disabilities in advocacy for financial support of needed services.

Klein (1991) has said that we learn about our differences so that we can build on our similarities. A preference that is clearly held in common by those in aging and independent living is allowing for choice and preference. Perhaps that is a more productive focus for discussion than is debating the merits of the independent living movement or of more family and medical care, for example. Indeed, younger adults advocate for broader application of the independent living movement in order to have the choices for which they fought in their youth available to them as they age.

* * *

Nancy N. Eustis, Ph.D., is professor of public affairs and planning at the University of Minnesota's Humphrey Institute of Public Affairs. Lucy Rose Fischer, Ph.D., is senior research scientist, Wilder Research Center, St. Paul, Minn.

REFERENCES

Antonucci, T. C., 1990. "Social Support and Social Relationships." In R. H. Binstock and L. K. George, eds., *Handbook of Aging and the Social Sciences,* 3d edition. San Diego, Calif.: Academic Press.

Batavia, A. I., DeJong, G. and McKnew, L. B., 1991. "Toward a National Personal Assistance Program: The Independent Living Model of Long Term Care for Persons with Disabilities." *Journal of Health Politics, Policy and Law* 16(3): 523–45.

Benjamin, A. E., 1989. "Chronic Care: Perspectives on Age and Aging." *Generations* 8(4): 19–22.

Budde, J., 1990. "Independent Living Rehabilitation: Concepts and Practices." In S. J. Brody and L. G. Pawlson, eds. *Aging and Rehabilitation II.* New York: Springer.

Chappell, N. L., 1990. "Aging and Social Care." In R. H. Binstock and L. K. George, eds., *Handbook of Aging and the Social Sciences,* 3d edition. San Diego, Calif.: Academic Press.

Cole, J. A., 1987. "Skills Training." In N. N. Crewe and I. K. Zola, eds., *Independent Living for Physically Disabled People.* San Francisco, Calif.: Jossey-Bass.

DeJong, G. and Wenker, T., 1987. "Attendant Care." In N. N. Crewe and I. K. Zola, eds., *Independent Living for Physically Disabled People.* San Francisco: Jossey-Bass.

DeJong, G., Batavia, A. I. and McKnew, L. B., 1992. "The Independent Living Model of Personal Assistance in National Long-Term-Care Policy." *Generations* 16 (1):89 (herein, Chapter 20, p. 177).

Eustis, N. N. and Fischer, L. R., 1991. "Relationships Between Homecare Clients and their Workers: Implications for Quality Care." *Gerontologist* 31(4): 447–56.

Eustis, N., Greenberg, J. and Patten, S., 1984. *Long-Term Care for Older Persons: A Policy Perspective.* Belmont, Calif.: Brooks/Cole.

Fischer, L. R. and Eustis, N. N., in press. "Care at Home: Family Caregivers and Home Care Workers." In E. Kahana and D. Biegel, eds., *Family Caregiving Across the Lifespan.* Beverly Hills, Calif.: Sage.

Fischer, L. R. et al., 1989. *Older Minnesotans: What Do They Need? How Do They Contribute?* St. Paul, Minn.: Senior Study, Wilder Research Center.

Hanley, R. J., Wiener, J. M. and Harris, K. M., 1991. "Will Paid Home Care Erode Informal Support?" *Journal of Health Politics, Policy, and Law* 16(3): 507–22.

Heumann, J. E., 1986. "The Independent Living Movement: Benefits for the Elderly." *Toward a Unified Agenda: Proceedings of a National Conference on Disability and Aging.* San Francisco, Calif.: Institute for Health and Aging, University of California.

Heumann, J. E., 1991. "Presentation Before the Senate Committee on Labor and Human Resources," in *Personal Assistance Services: A Guide To Policy and Action.* Oakland, Calif.: World Institute on Disability.

Hofland, B., ed., 1990. "Autonomy and Long-Term-Care Practice." *Generations* 14 (Supplement).

Justice, D., 1988. *State Long Term Care Reform: Development of Community Care Systems in Six States.* Washington, D.C.: Health Policy Studies, Center for Policy Research, National Governors Association.

Kailes, J. I., 1992. "Aging with a Disability: Educating Myself." *Generations* 16(1):75 (herein, Chapter 17, p. 149).

Kane, R. A. and Kane, R. L., 1987. *Long-Term Care: Principles, Programs and Policies.* New York: Springer.

Kane, R. L., 1991. Interview conducted by N. Eustis.

Kimmich, M. H., 1991. "Consumer-Directed Personal Assistance Services: How Do the Elderly Fare?" *Disabilities Studies Quarterly* 11(4):17–19.

Klein, D., 1991. "Presentation of a Unified Agenda for Disabled Persons of All Ages: Moving from Concept to Reality." Presentation at the 44th Annual Scientific Meeting of the Gerontoogical Society of America. San Francisco, Calif., Nov.

Litvak, S. and Kennedy, J., 1991. *Policy Issues Affecting the Medicaid Personal Care Services Optional Benefit.* Oakland, Calif.: World Institute on Disability.

Litvak, S., Heumann, J. and Zukas, H., 1987. *Attending to America: Personal Assistance for Independent Living.* Oakland, Calif.: World Institute on Disability.

Litwak, E., 1985. *Helping the Elderly.* New York: Guilford Press.

Mahoney, C. W., 1986. "Epilogue." *Toward a Unified Agenda: Proceedings of a National Conference on Disability and Aging.* San Francisco, Calif.: Institute for Health and Aging, University of California.

Management Group, 1990. *What Is Quality in Long Term Care? The Customer's View.* Long Term Support Quality Initiative Series, Document 3. Madison, Wis.

Racino, J. A. and Heumann, J. E., 1992. "Independent Living and Community Life: Building Coalitions Among Elders, People with Disabilities, and Our Allies." *Generations* 16(1):43 (herein, Chapter 9, p. 79).

Reif, L., 1990. "Consumers Speak Out About Home Care." *Aging Connection,* August/September, p. 5.

Sabatino, C. P., 1990. *Final Report: Lessons for Enhancing Consumer-Directed Approaches in Home Care.* Washington, D.C.: Commission on Legal Problems of the Elderly, American Bar Association.

Sabatino, C. P. and Litvak, S., 1992. "Consumer-Directed Homecare: What Makes It Possible?" *Generations* 16(1):53 (herein, Chapter 11, p. 99).

Simon-Rusinowitz, L. and Hofland, B. F, pending. "The Impact of Varying Perspectives on Client Autonomy in Long Term Care: Home Care for the Elderly vs. Attendant Services for the Disabled." (Submitted to *Gerontologist.*)

Vivona, V. and Kaplan, D., 1990. "People with Developmental Disabilities Speak Out on Quality of Life." Oakland, Calif.: World Institute on Disability.

Zola, I. K., 1988, "Policies and Programs Concerning Aging and Disability: Toward a Unified Agenda." In S. Sullivan and M. Einlewin, eds., *The Economics and Ethics of Long-Term Care and Disability.* Washington, D.C.: American Enterprise Institute for Public Policy Research, pp. 90–130.

REHABILITATION SERVICES FOR ELDERS

Chapter 4

Aging and Rehabilitation: Beyond the Medical Model

Stanley J. Brody and Malcolm H. Morrison

To go beyond the medical model requires recognition that the combined effects of demography and the increase in medical knowledge and health services delivery bring rehabilitation to the forefront of care for the aging.

Living Americans of every age are more likely than people in any previous time in history to reach old age and even "old-old" age. With this new phenomenon of life expectancy we have achieved an "aging society," with different expectations, experiences, and aspirations.

It is well to repeat that at the beginning of this century, life expectancy had doubled over 2,400 years of previous history. Thus, an individual born in 1900 could expect to live 43 years, a little more than twice that in biblical times. Today, less than 100 years later, life expectancy has now been lengthened by 33 years, one and a half times the extension that occurred during the previous 24 centuries.

Absorbing this information is difficult enough, but the old person today presents a picture different from that presented even three decades ago. Then we collected data reflecting the goals of a health system that focused successfully on acute care and life extension. Our health was described solely in terms of mortality and morbidity, of death and disease.

Studies at mid-century suggested that our new health problems were those of chronic care rather than only acute care, but even these data were presented in terms of disease—chronic rather than acute (Brody, 1973). It was not until the sixties that new descriptions were provided to characterize aging.

Instead of focusing exclusively on chronological age, the new dimension of *functioning* was introduced into our treatment and data collection approach. The Activities of Daily Living (ADL) (Katz et al., 1963) and the Instrumental Activities of Daily Living (IADL) (Lawton and E. Brody, 1969) concepts allowed us to shift the focus in evaluating health problems of the aging from one of acute care and life extension to chronic care and quality of life. While slow to develop, federal data-gathering agencies (e.g., the National Center for Health Statistics and the Census Bureau) have in the last ten years reflected this movement from an exclusive acute-care orientation (using mortality and morbidity measures) to a chronic illness and disability focus (using data on impairments and functional capacity).

The significant increase in length of life and recognition of the importance of functional capacity can be viewed as the first two stages in the development of a new view of continuity of care.

Following closely was a third stage, which expanded on the concept of "an aging society" (Binstock, 1986) and appreciation of "chronic care as a major health problem of this generation" (Brody, 1973). This stage involved differentiating among the elderly in terms of functional capability. Again, Sidney Katz led conceptually by defining the category of "active life expectancy" to distinguish among the burgeoning groups of the aged whose life expectancy at age 65 had increased more than 20 percent since 1965 (Katz et al., 1983). By "active" he was describing those elders who were free of ADL deficits.

This third stage saw the appearance of reliable data that described a new and changing elderly population. Added to the growing awareness of the "old-old" population—the increasing number of people over age 85—was the projection that there will be over a million centenarians by the mid-twenty-first century. Moreover, this aging society seems to be healthy, with 76 percent of the elderly being described as functionally independent. While men at age 65 could look forward to 12 more years of an active lifestyle and women 13-1/2 years, even those of

85 years could look forward to three more years of active life expectancy (Manton and Stalland, 1991).

Of those older persons with functional limitations, 6.7 percent have Instrumental Activities of Daily Living deficits only; 8.2 percent have one or two Activities of Daily Living deficits; 4.3 percent have three or four such deficits; and 4.6 percent, the severely disabled, have five or six deficits. Even in this last group, nearly twice as many live in the community as in nursing homes.

The fourth stage of conceptual understanding developed the challenging idea that older persons with disabilities were not in a cycle of inevitable and continuous decline. When the "active life expectancy" concept emerged, disabling impairments were seen as the predecessor of decline in health and functional status, leading to death. This view is now recognized as a "false stereotype" (Branch et al., 1991). New data, provided by successive national surveys of the elderly population focusing on the prevalence of disability, have now confirmed clinical experiences with small samples showing that there are a substantial number of elderly disabled who regain a greater degree of independence (Manton, 1988). Thus, what emerges from research on the differences among the elderly population is that interventions must have the ultimate goal not only of increasing longevity but also of reducing disability (Guralnick et al., 1991).

The recognition that older persons with disabilities are not automatically at risk for decline and can regain and retain functional capacity has led to the fifth stage of understanding rehabilitation for the aging population. The Institute of Medicine's Committee on a National Research Agenda on Aging recently published its report—*Extending Life, Enhancing Life* (Institute of Medicine, 1991). In outlining goals for clinical research, the committee focused on "research into the causes, prevention, management and rehabilitation of disability in older persons" and established this as its first priority (pp. 57–58). The committee went on to suggest that research should be conducted on the interacting effects of age, lifestyle factors, and diseases on the disability status of older persons. This priority was also supported by the "Behavioral and Social Sciences" section, which noted that "from this knowledge of differential approaches to old age, stems the concept of modifiability of aging" (p. 74). Following up on this idea it was observed that "despite the recognition that the major health problems of older people are chronic, little attention has been paid to behavioral and social interventions to reduce excessive disability and provide new treatment and management strategies. Some key issues for researchers include rehabilitative strategies to maintain or restore function, treatment of the social or emotional barriers to rehabilitation, and compliance with medical regimens" (p. 76).

Further, in endorsing the need for research into long-term care and continuity of care for older persons, the "Health Services Delivery Research" section of the report affirmed the focus on enhancing the ability of the elderly to live independently (p. 101). This reflects the objectives of long-term care established in 1980 by a Department of Health and Human Services committee headed by Ethel Shanas: "to help older persons cope with their disabilities, decrease dependence on others and narrow the gap between actual and potential functioning" (U.S. Department of Health and Human Services, 1980).

We are beginning to understand the characteristics of chronic disabilities and the accompanying need for continuity of care approaches involving collaboration among formal and informal service providers using case management and assessment, treatment, and caregiving beyond the medical model.

But there is little evidence of concern in acute care medical settings with a multidisciplinary approach to rehabilitation for older persons with disabilities. The goal is to "cure" the patient and obtain reimbursement under the DRG system, which is itself focused on disease or specific conditions.

At present, a few healthcare organizations are using a multidisciplinary approach, and for the most part they are rehabilitation hospitals and comprehensive outpatient rehabilitation facilities (CORFs). Today, with the developing incentives for "managed care," some of these providers are extending their services to older persons in two directions: intervening earlier in the impairment episode, even when it is still in an acute phase; and continuing to provide services on an outpatient basis *and in the community,* after discharge from a rehabilitation hospital (or rehabilitation unit in a general hospital). In a few instances, hospitals with rehabilitation resources are boldly experimenting with "complete" treatment approaches, beginning with acute care geriatric treatment, followed by inpatient and outpatient rehabilitation, and then services provided in the person's residence. In some cases, rehabilitation hospitals have established comprehensive geriatric *rehabilitation* teams that work with the older person and family members to ensure successful rehabilitation outcomes and continuity of care.

In general though, there is very little public or private support for these types of more coordinated care, oriented toward improving and maintaining the functions of individuals at home, in the community, or in other residential settings. Despite much discussion of the need for more integrated care and despite clear recognition that the acute medical model cannot be used to achieve this goal, reimbursement, professional practice, and health systems delivery incentives are still not structured to encourage coordination and continuity of care. There is hardly any recognition that the focus of care must change from disease to impairment and disability, from illness to function, from acute care to rehabilitation. The important challenge for rehabilitation and geriatrics is to produce new models of continuity of care that will incorporate the multiple services available to improve and maintain *function* for older persons with chronic impairments.

Neither the education of physicians—nor that of other health personnel or operating healthcare systems—subscribes to goals expressed in terms of the patient's function. Chronic care receives scant attention in medical school curricula, and medical specialties increasingly focus on the disease rather than the person as a whole. Family practitioners and geriatricians are those most likely to focus on the elderly's needs for continuity of care, as are rehabilitation hospitals and comprehensive outpatient programs.

Yet, geriatricians are often uncomfortable in acknowledging the need to use resources beyond acute medical care. The "geriatric team," almost always limited to the geriatrician, nurse, and social worker, ignores the rehabilitation group of occupational, physical, audiological, and speech therapists and physiatrists. There is evidence that the two fields of physical medicine/rehabilitation and geriatrics as medical specialties have followed separate, isolated yet parallel paths, with interaction limited by professional protection issues. Lack of cooperation may also have an economic basis, since reimbursement for geriatric medical services differs from that of rehabilitation services provided to the very same patients. This is one more example of why it is so difficult to achieve a system that will focus on the management of chronic disabilities based on improvement and maintenance of functional capacity.

Healthcare reimbursement remains focused almost entirely on acute care and on particular physician, hospital, or long-term-care providers. Establishing a healthcare delivery system appropriate for chronic disability management will require a more collaborative approach involving multiple healthcare providers in the community working with families in assisting them to choose appropriate acute, transitional, and long-term-care options. Developing effective delivery mechanisms and reimbursement incentives that enable use of multiple treatment settings (including the home environment) is the key challenge for both geriatrics and rehabilitation. If management of chronic disability is to focus on functional restoration, then the healthcare system must be organized to achieve this goal by coordinating interventions with the individual in a continuous process where the type, amount, intensity, location(s), and providers of services will vary with the needs of the individual. A critical care medical intervention model is not compatible with the continuity of care required by the chronically disabled.

Rehabilitation emerges as a significant element in both research and clinical practice agendas in the 1990s and beyond. The natural history of disability over time represents an emphasis that looks at the interface of lifestyles with disease, together with the environment and other psychosocial factors that may begin during youth and middle age. Rehabilitation intervention is often the "glue" that links acute, transitional, and long-term-care systems, so that continuity of care may maximize the functioning of the elderly disabled.

The challenge to an aging society is to support a concept of health that focuses on the quality of life within the context of a system that offers economic incentives to providers to be "user friendly."

* * *

Stanley J. Brody, J.D., M.S.W., is professor emeritus of Physical Medicine and Rehabilitation in Psychiatry, School of Medicine; professor emeritus of Health Care Systems, Wharton School of Finance and Commerce; and former director of the Center for Rehabilitation of Elderly and Disabled Individuals at the University of Pennsylvania. Malcolm H. Morrison, Ph.D., is director of research and program development, National Association of Rehabilitation Facilities, Reston, Va., and professorial lecturer in aging, Graduate School of Arts and Sciences, George Washington University, Washington, D.C.

REFERENCES

Binstock, R., 1986. "Aging and Rehabilitation: The Birth of a Social Movement." In S. Brody and G. Ruff, eds., *Aging and Rehabilitation*. New York: Springer.

Branch, L. G. et al., 1991. "Active Life Expectancy for 10,000 Caucasian Men and Women in Three Communities." *Journal of Gerontology, Medical Sciences* 46(4):145–50.

Brody, S. J., 1973. "Comprehensive Health Care for the Elderly: An Analysis (The Continuum of Medical, Health and Social Services for Aging)." *Gerontologist* 13(4): 412–18.

Guralnick, J. M. et al., 1991. "Morbidity and Disability in Older Persons in the Years Prior to Death." *American Journal of Public Health* 81: 443–47.

Institute of Medicine, Committee on a National Research Agenda on Aging, 1991. *Extending Life, Enhancing Life: A National Research Agenda on Aging,* E. T. Lonergan, ed. Washington, D.C.: National Academy of Sciences.

Katz S. et al., 1963. "Studies of Illness in the Aged: The Index of ADL: A Standardized Measure of Biological and Psychosocial Function." *Journal of the American Medical Association* 185:914–19.

Katz, S. et al., 1983. "Active Life Expectancy." *New England Journal of Medicine* 309(20):1218–29.

Lawton, P. and Brody, E., 1969. "Assessment of Older People: Self-Maintaining and Instruments of Daily Living." *Gerontologist* 9: 179–86.

Manton, K. G., 1988. "Longitudinal Study of Functional Change and Mortality in the United States." *Journal of Gerontology, Social Sciences* 43(8):153– 61.

Manton, K. G. and Stalland, E., 1991. "Cross-Sectional Estimates of Active Life Expectancy of the U.S. Elderly and Oldest-Old Populations." *Journal of Gerontology, Social Sciences* 46(3):170–82.

U.S. Department of Health and Human Services, 1980. "Report of the National Committee on Vital and Health Statistics. Long Term Health Care Minimum Data Set." DHHS Publication Number (PHS) 80-1158. Hyattsville, Md.: Office of Research Statistics and Technology, National Center for Health Statistics.

Chapter 5

Geriatric Rehabilitation

Kenneth Brummel-Smith

Rehabilitation is the process whereby persons with functional deficits can be assisted either to adapt to the deficits or to recover certain capabilities. Most medical practitioners view rehabilitation as appropriate for a person who has suffered a stroke or amputation. However, the philosophical basis of rehabilitation is appropriate in all aspects of care of geriatric patients, because older persons are more likely to develop functional deficits, even after a simple hospitalization (Warshaw et al., 1982). Although this chapter will address specific rehabilitation programs, it should be remembered that all geriatric care must be oriented to preserving and enhancing function.

PRINCIPLES OF REHABILITATION

The basic principles of rehabilitation are the same regardless of the client's age (List 1). However, there are a number of important differences in the application of those principles when one is working with older clients. One method for viewing these differences will be presented here. There are other ways to describe these differences (Brummel-Smith, 1990a).

Stabilizing the primary disorder is more difficult—and sometimes impossible—in older persons, since they frequently have more than one primary problem. For example, it would be difficult to establish the primary disorder for a stroke patient who also suffers from

Principles of Rehabilitation

Stabilize the primary problem

Prevent secondary disabilities

Treat functional deficits

Promote adaption:

- person to disability
- environment to person
- family to person

List 1

hypertension and diabetes. Furthermore, what exactly is "stable"? It is unfortunately too common to see older patients stay for extended periods of time in acute care hospitals awaiting this elusive stability before being transferred for rehabilitation. Geriatric rehabilitation programs typically accept patients while their medical problems are still being stabilized.

Preventing secondary disabilities is also more difficult in the older client. These complications (List 2) occur more frequently than they do in younger persons—and may be more difficult to treat. For instance, older people are more prone to pressure sores. They are also more likely to develop malnutrition or suffer adverse drug reactions from anticoagulants given to prevent deep venous thrombosis. Constant vigilance to prevent medical, psychological, and social complications is necessary.

Whether there are differences in the actual treatment for restoration of lost functional capabilities in older persons is controversial. Elderly clients have a slower learning pace and may require more frequent repetitions than a younger person. However, it appears from clinical experience that there are no outstanding differences in the acquisition of new functional skills simply based upon age.

Finally, the promotion of adaptation is the cornerstone of rehabilitation. Adaptation must occur in a number of areas. The person must first adapt to his or her disability. Such a process requires many

Secondary Disabilities

Anorexia	Incontinence
Aspiration	Malnutrition
Confusion	Pneumonia
Contractures	Pressure Sores
Deconditioning	Psychologic dependency
Depression	Venous thrombosis

List 2

months—sometimes years. It is unclear whether this process is affected by aging. Some practitioners have spoken of a "right to dependency," describing an attitude in which older persons believe that because of their age, it is their right to be taken care of by others. My own experience is that this phenomenon is infrequently encountered. More often older persons may overestimate their capacity to function at a level consistent with safety.

The environment, too, must be adapted to the person. Assistive devices, such as walkers or wheelchairs, place certain requirements on the environment. Doors may need to be widened. Ramps may need to be installed. Such modifications are expensive and not covered by Medicare. Older persons may not want to have their homes modified. Transportation services for disabled older persons may not be available in the community.

Last, the family must be helped to adapt to the person's new capabilities. Because family support is the key to successful rehabilitation outcomes, working closely with and supporting family members is a vital component of geriatric rehabilitation. The family members may be quite old themselves and limited in their ability to do lifting or assist with transfers. Children may be unavailable or overprotective (another form of the belief in a "right to dependency"). There may be significant preexisting family problems that are magnified by the stress of assisting a disabled older person (Corgiat, 1988). Thus, for myriad reasons, family conferences should be held frequently when dealing with elderly clients.

REHABILITATION TEAMS

Rehabilitation teams in geriatrics usually contain those members listed in List 3.

An in-depth discussion of the duties of each type of practitioner can be found elsewhere (Brummel-Smith, 1990b). When working with geriatric clients, however, there are some special considerations. Psychologists play an important role in assessing the client for both depression and cognitive deficits, two conditions found much more frequently in elderly patients (Garcia et al., 1984; Gans, 1981). All team members must be sensitive to the possibility that the patient is depressed—not merely "poorly motivated." Team members must be aware that older persons learn more slowly and may have negative attitudes about their ability to recover after suffering a major disability (Kemp, 1990). Even small gains may be interpreted as a great achievement by the older person; it is thus important for team members to include the patient's assessment of his or her progress when developing goals. Because the original goal of rehabilitation was of return to work, geriatric rehabilitation teams must view return to an independent lifestyle and development of avocational skills as worthwhile goals. Finally, as many older persons have significant underlying cardiopulmonary disorders, physical and occupational therapists must be able to monitor physiologic status during therapy.

When working with older clients, teams often find that their roles overlap. Nurses may counsel patients, therapists may detect depression, social workers may observe cognitive changes and suggest that a

Rehabilitation Team Members

Physician	Vocational counselor
Nurse	Recreational therapist
Occupational therapist	Psychologist
Physical therapist	Speech pathologist
Social worker	Consultants

List 3

medication problem may be the cause. Because rehabilitation of older clients is more difficult, it is important for all members not to miss any opportunity to help the patient improve. Belief that any single discipline "owns" a particular part of the treatment has no place in geriatric rehabilitation. It is particularly important for the physician to be sensitive to this fact.

SETTINGS FOR REHABILITATION

While the classic site of rehabilitation may be the acute rehabilitation unit or hospital, many other sites are often used when working with older persons (List 4). The rehabilitation unit is still the best place for someone with a recent, significant disability who has the ability to undergo up to three hours of therapy per day and who needs close medical supervision. Medicare reimbursement is generally available for most conditions as long as these requirements are met and the client makes demonstrable progress toward goals. Rehabilitation interventions can occur in the acute hospital as well. However, with the shortened stays seen since the advent of prospective payment, most such interventions should be designed to prevent functional losses.

The skilled nursing facility (SNF) is appropriate for the patient who cannot tolerate the intensive treatment provided in an acute "rehab" unit. In one study, 57 percent of clients undergoing rehabilitation in an SNF were able to return home (Alderman, 1987). Medicare-certified facilities must have therapists on staff, and clients must be shown to make progress toward goals (not merely be "maintained"). Unfortunately, many SNFs have not made rehabilitation a priority.

Sites for Rehabilitation

- Acute rehabilitation unit
- Skilled nursing facility
- Outpatient rehabilitation clinic
- Home

List 4

Adequate space and therapeutic equipment may not be available, and the staff may not include physicians knowledgeable in rehabilitation.

Outpatient rehabilitation clinics may be appropriate for the patient with less severe deficits. While space and equipment may not be a problem, the key limiting factor is often the client's transportation needs. Clinics offer the opportunity to mix with other people recovering from disability. For some this will be seen as a challenge, while for others it may be intimidating. Some communities offer services through Certified Outpatient Rehabilitation Facilities (CORF).

The client's home is an ideal site for many older persons to receive rehabilitation. Newly learned techniques like transfers or cooking skills can be tested in the client's real environment. Transportation is not a problem. Family training may be more easily accomplished. For properly chosen patients, the services can be rendered at a cost lower than that in the hospital (Jarnio et al., 1984).

PROBLEM AREAS IN GERIATRIC REHABILITATION

Geriatrics is a relatively new area in medicine. Geriatric rehabilitation, as a distinct entity, is even newer. As a result there are many problematic features in the field. Three of these will be addressed here: (1) the best way to measure rehabilitation potential, (2) the lack of controlled trials demonstrating effectiveness of the approach, and (3) issues regarding costs and cost-containment.

Before acceptance into a geriatric rehabilitation program (regardless of the site of care), the client's potential for benefiting from care must be assessed. Rehabilitation is one of the few areas in medicine where the providers essentially control access to services in that they make judgments about rehabilitation potential. This has significant ethical and medical implications. First, the patient's need for rehabilitation may not be recognized. This is a particular concern when dealing with older clients because of ageist concepts that may lead providers to view disability as "expected" with advanced age. Second, many nonmedical factors are often involved in the selection process. Financial considerations, the availability of support in the home, and insurance status have a strong effect on the decisions of rehabilitation providers. Finally, should clients' contribution to their disability affect the decision? Does the active alcoholic who had a leg amputated because of self-neglect have the same right to rehabilitation as the stroke victim?

The medical aspects of evaluation for rehabilitation potential are also unclear. To date no controlled trials have evaluated an assessment method for determining potential. All studies so far have tested the reliability of a particular instrument, such as the Barthel index (Granger et al., 1977), in predicting outcomes *after* a patient had been accepted to a program. While most providers use a combination of standardized assessments and clinical acumen, the process is strikingly subjective.

There is a similar lack of randomized, controlled trials in measuring outcomes of different types of rehabilitation interventions and in different sites of care (Kane, 1990). Studies are needed that measure outcomes, the effect of different types of interventions, the impact of the involvement of different types of providers, and effective use of the treatment team. More attention should be paid to the natural history of disability. How much recovery of lost function do people develop as a result of their rehabilitation versus the simple passage of time? Does a period of rehabilitation allow for more positive changes once the program has been completed? To what degree should social resources be considered in the selection process, and should outcomes be measured in terms of physical functional capabilities or by the more important aspects of social functioning? In this era of cost-containment, the answer to these types of questions will become more important.

Finally, there is the issue of cost and cost-containment. Rehabilitation is expensive. It has been estimated that the average cost of rehabilitation for a spinal cord injury is $500,000. When viewed from a vocational rehabilitation model, one might argue that these costs are "worth it" because the person will be returning to work. But in geriatrics the emphasis shifts to an "independent living" model where the likelihood of returning to work is minimal. It remains to be seen whether the specter of rationing of care will be applied to rehabilitation. Currently, inpatient rehabilitation programs are exempt from the prospective payment system. As healthcare costs continue to mount, it seems likely that some form of restriction on payments will be on the horizon.

* * *

Kenneth Brummel-Smith, M.D., is associate professor of medicine and family medicine, Division of Geriatrics, Department of Medicine, Portland VA Medical Center, Portland, Oregon.

REFERENCES

Alderman, R. D., 1987. "A Community-oriented Geriatric Rehabilitation Unit in a Nursing Home." *Gerontologist* 27:143–46.

Brummel-Smith, K., 1990a. "Introduction." in B. Kemp, K. Brummel-Smith and J. W. Ramsdell, eds., *Geriatric Rehabilitation.* Boston, Mass.: College-Hill Press, pp. 3–21.

Brummel-Smith K., 1990b. "Rehabilitation." in C. K. Cassell, et al., eds., *Geriatric Medicine.* New York: Springer-Verlag, 125–40.

Corgiat, M. D., 1988. "Identifying Dysfunctional Families in Geriatric Rehabilitation." *Topics in Geriatric Rehabilitation* 4(1):16–24.

Gans, J. S., 1981. "Depression Diagnosis in a Rehabilitation Hospital." *Archives of Physical Medicine and Rehabilitation* 62:386–89.

Garcia, C. A., Tweedy, J. R. and Blass, J.P., 1984. "Underdiagnosis of Cognitive Impairment in a Rehabilitation Setting." *Journal of the American Geriatric Society* 32:339–42.

Granger, C., Sherwood, C. and Greer, D., 1977. "Functional Status Measures in a Comprehensive Stroke Care Program." *Archives of Physical Medicine and Rehabilitation* 58:555–61.

Jarnio, G.B., Ceder, L. and Thorngren, K.G., 1984. "Early Rehabilitation at Home of Elderly Patients with Hip Fracture and Consumption of Resources in Primary Care." *Scandinavian Journal of Primary Health Care* 2:105–12.

Kane, R.L. 1990. "Measuring the Effectiveness of Rehabilitation Programs." In B. Kemp, K. Brummel-Smith and J. W. Ramsdell, eds., *Geriatric Rehabilitation,* Boston, Mass.: College-Hill Press, pp. 429–40.

Kemp, B., 1990. "The Psychosocial Context of Geriatric Rehabilitation." In B. Kemp, K. Brummel-Smith and J. W. Ramsdell, eds., *Geriatric Rehabilitation.* Boston, Mass.: College-Hill Press, pp. 41–60.

Warshaw, G. et al., 1982. "Functional Disability in the Hospitalized Elderly." *Journal of the American Medical Association* 248:847–50.

Chapter 6

Availability of Rehabilitation Services for Elders: A Study of Critical Policy and Financing Issues*

Linda A. Wray and Fernando M. Torres-Gil

Current research supports the need for and effectiveness of rehabilitation services for older as well as younger persons with disabilities (see, for example, Branch et al., 1984; Kane et al., 1984; Brody and Ruff, 1986; Brody and Pawlson, 1990; Kemp et al., 1990; Kovar and Feinleib, 1991). Nevertheless, programs to promote rehabilitation services for the elderly are relatively absent in existing legislation; acute illnesses rather than chronic conditions are emphasized in health service reimbursement; and professionals in the rehabilitation and aging fields continue to fragment their advocacy efforts.

This chapter presents findings of a recent study that examines these critical policy and financing issues. In the first section, the dearth of existing public policy concerning the rehabilitation needs of older persons is described and the limited legislative efforts extending chronic care benefits to the elderly are examined. Findings of congressional and state agency surveys are discussed in the following section. Finally, the policy implications of this research are explored.

*This research was conducted by the Rancho Los Amigos Rehabilitation Research and Training Center on Aging and the University of Southern California, and was supported in part by the National Institute on Disability and Rehabilitation Research of the U.S. Department of Education.

GERIATRIC REHABILITATION POLICY TODAY

Rehabilitation aims to improve, restore, or maintain functioning in order to promote maximum independence in persons with chronic conditions. In older persons, these chronic conditions may be single or multiple and may be the result of later-life effects of developmental or childhood disabilities, or later-life accidents or diseases. The disabling conditions may result in loss of function or ability to care for oneself at home, to carry out activities in the community, to work, or to fulfill social roles. Geriatric rehabilitation is the application of the principles of rehabilitation to the chronic disabling conditions of later life, taking into account the unique biological, psychological, and social characteristics of the older person.

Currently, the availability of rehabilitative services aimed at older persons with chronic disabling conditions is disproportionate to the needs of the growing elderly population. Existing public policies provide limited incentives for a continuum of institutional and noninstitutional, age-related, and multidisciplinary rehabilitation services. The inherent ageism in many policies and services is based on the faulty assumption by policy makers and healthcare providers that older people are difficult to rehabilitate because their functioning cannot improve (Benedict and Ganikos, 1981; Becker and Kaufman, 1988; Kane and Kane, 1990; Kemp et al., 1990).

In short, the dilemma of public rehabilitation programs for older persons with chronic disabilities can be viewed as an interaction of inconsistent research data and existing rehabilitation policies and financing mechanisms.

Inconsistent Research Findings

Current literature indicates that while people are living longer, they may not be living healthier (Verbrugge, 1984, 1989, 1991; Crimmins et al., 1989; Olshansky et al., 1991). Fortunately, longitudinal studies demonstrate that functional inability among the older populations may be reversible and that the factors associated with functional loss differ from those associated with functional improvement (Branch et al., 1984; Manton, 1988; Branch and Ku, 1989; Crimmins and Saito, 1990). Such studies support claims that many disabling conditions—in both older and younger persons—may be prevented or improved with medical, rehabilitation, and lifestyle interventions (Verbrugge, 1984, 1989).

The data also project that the volume of chronic disabling conditions will increase in the future. At the same time, fertility, labor force, geographic mobility, and informal family support patterns suggest that fewer persons may be available in the home as caregivers, increasing the demand for formal institutional and community- or home-based long-term and rehabilitative care. Thus, preventing or postponing functional disability among older people is increasingly cited as an important public health goal (Kovar and Feinleib, 1991). However, how dependency and disability should be reduced most effectively and efficiently is still in question.

For example, two decades of federally sponsored demonstration programs have investigated the substitutability of community-based long-term care for institutional (e.g., nursing home and hospital) services. Analyses of the demonstration data provide uneven findings. In particular, evidence of cost-effectiveness of community-based care is inconsistent. However, the data do support increased quality of life and a strong preference for noninstitutional care by both elderly and non-elderly people with disabilities (see, for example, Weissert, 1985, 1988; Leutz et al., 1988; Price and O'Shaughnessy, 1990; Torres-Gil and Rosenquist, 1990).

Other small-scale cross-sectional studies testing the effectiveness of individual restorative strategies found similar levels of functional improvement for older as well as younger persons, although the duration of rehabilitation may have been somewhat longer for the elderly (Kane et al., 1984; Brody and Ruff, 1986; Kemp et al., 1990). Given that the functional improvements often resulted in reduced dependency and delayed institutionalization, researchers have suggested that rehabilitation may be cost-effective in the long-run for at least some disabling conditions (Anderson et al., 1979; Johnston and Keith, 1983; Granger, 1986; Binstock, 1990). Unfortunately, evidence of cost-effectiveness is still limited: Assessment tools and outcomes measures for rehabilitation techniques are not widely accepted (Frymoyer, 1986; Kane, 1990), and hard data from large-scale longitudinal studies are not yet available.

Policies and Financing

Currently, more than 80 federal and many state and local programs offer some level of assistance for long-term care and rehabilitation needs (U.S. House of Representatives, 1986, 1988; GAO, 1989; Price and O'Shaughnessy, 1990). Such assistance includes Supplemental Security Income and Social Security Disability Insurance benefits to eligible older or disabled persons, Older Americans Act home-delivered meals for older persons who are housebound, and case management services under some Medicaid state option programs. However, program objectives, definitions of disability, eligibility criteria, and reimbursement schemes vary widely and interact unevenly across programs. For example, eligibility can be based on age, financial need, functional impairment, or impoverishment resulting from large medical expenditures.

These programs can be seen as existing within two parallel but separate public policy streams that emerged during the twentieth century. The term "geriatric rehabilitation" is a good descriptor for both. Myriad laws target services to individuals who are older—the geriatric stream—or to individuals who have disabilities—the rehabilitation stream. Programs within the geriatric stream were not designed to promote rehabilitation for older persons.

For example, Medicare was established to provide episodic acute care—primarily in institutional settings—rather than longer-term chronic care in noninstitutional settings. While Medicare currently reimburses retrospectively for selected medical rehabilitation services, generally the services must be deemed "reasonable and necessary" and must be ordered by a physician, and the condition must be expected to improve with therapy. However, the existing diagnosis-related group and prospective payment systems for acute care provide disincentives for physicians to keep older persons in hospitals, in turn furthering the disincentives to order the available in-hospital rehabilitation services. To date, Medicare does not reimburse for preventive physical therapy, and only under limited circumstances for maintenance physical therapy.

The rehabilitation stream was established to provide supportive services to injured veterans, encourage their independent living, and promote vocational or work-life potential. While the Rehabilitation Act of 1973 broadened the scope of rehabilitation services beyond the traditional vocational focus, most programs continue to center on work-life potential and generally younger clientele. In fact, limited data indicate that fewer than 10 percent of beneficiaries of programs operated by state Departments of Rehabilitation are over age 55 (Benedict and Ganikos, 1981; Cromar, 1984). Thus, an artificial dichotomy remains in effect between policies affecting older and younger persons with disabilities.

In contrast, the 1990 Americans with Disabilities Act represents a first step by policy makers in addressing issues affecting disabled persons of all ages. In addition, recent limited federal efforts mark a shift away from the traditional model of healthcare based on age and acute conditions, and a move toward a more flexible model based on functional status and chronic conditions. For example, based on the research and recommendations of the 1990 Pepper Commission report, the final 1990 budget reconciliation package gives states the option under Medicaid to offer selected home- and community-based services (e.g., personal care, adult day healthcare) to selected low-income elderly people. Services will be available to persons who are functionally disabled and at risk for nursing home care, according to state-designated interdisciplinary assessment teams.

GERIATRIC REHABILITATION POLICY SURVEYS

Researchers at the University of Southern California recently explored the availability of public rehabilitation services for older persons in two sets of interviews. In-person interviews were conducted in the summer of 1990 with 25 professional staff persons representing 21 congressional committees with jurisdiction over aging- and disability-related programs and issues. Telephone interviews were completed in the spring of 1991 with 38 representatives of aging, rehabilitation, health, and social services agencies in nine states (California, Connecticut, Florida, Iowa, Louisiana, Michigan, Minnesota, Oregon, and Virginia).

The congressional committee survey solicited the views of professional staff persons representing a nonrandom purposive sample of U.S. Senate and House of Representatives authorizing, financing, and advisory aging committees. Open-ended survey questions covered three subjects: general healthcare needs of older persons; geriatric rehabilitation needs, services, and outcomes; and barriers to providing geriatric rehabilitation services.

In selecting the agency interview sample, all states were initially ranked along three dimensions (1) characteristics of at-risk populations, (2) aging and disability/rehabilitation policy effort, and (3) economic well-being and general policy liberalism. Nine states were selected to exhibit geographic balance and maximum variation across the three dimensions. The sample was loaded heavily with states that showed high policy efforts despite low levels of at-risk populations or economic well-being. Interviews with senior agency staff were conducted in early 1991 in order to capture leadership and policy shifts as a result of the 1990 gubernatorial elections. Agency survey questions were largely close-ended, with potential responses based on findings from the congressional committee survey. (See Wray, 1991a, 1991b for more detailed discussions of these surveys.)

Briefly, the survey findings supported two of the three study hypotheses: (1) Obstacles in existing public programs and financing mechanisms narrow the provision of geriatric rehabilitation services, and (2) advocacy for such services by the aging and disability communities is limited.

The third hypothesis—that public officials have limited comprehensive knowledge of the needs and outcomes of geriatric rehabilitation services—was supported in interviews with congressional committee representatives but not in interviews with state agency staff. In fact, the state responses suggested that agency staff, and particularly rehabilitation agency staff, are perhaps more knowledgeable about needs and outcomes than are many policy makers at the federal level. In addition to testing these hypotheses, survey findings also pertain to perceived health needs and definitions of disability conditions and rehabilitation services.

Unmet Health Needs of Older Persons

In order to establish a general sense of perceived healthcare needs, respondents were asked to select the most critical unmet need of all older persons and all low-income older persons nationwide from a list that included the following: acute care, catastrophic healthcare, community- and home-based long-term care, institution-based long-term care, mental health services, rehabilitation services for chronic disabilities, treatment for Alzheimer's disease, and other needs. Most congressional and state agency respondents said community- and home-based long-term care is currently the most critical unmet health need.

When the list was expanded to include nonmedical services, over one-half reported that community- and home-based long-term care and in-home support services are the two main healthcare and supportive service needs of elders—now and in the future—that are currently not being met. Over half of the nonrehabilitation agency staff (but fewer than one-fifth of the rehabilitation agency staff) also cited supportive housing as one of the most critical unmet needs.

Defining Disabling Conditions and Rehabilitation Services

Nearly all congressional and state respondents agreed that traditional, non-age-specific disabling conditions (e.g., fractures, depression, and stroke) and traditional aging-related conditions (e.g., difficulties with activities of daily living, arthritis, Alzheimer's disease) rank highly in warranting rehabilitation services. Rehabilitation agency respondents were more likely than other federal or state respondents to cite disability due to childhood accidents or disease or to mental illness as also benefiting from rehabilitation strategies.

Respondents indicated that a comprehensive geriatric rehabilitation program should include a variety of health and support services. In particular, over half of the state agency respondents listed the following as necessary: physical or sensory impairment therapies; training in the use of assistive devices; in-home support; mental health, counseling, and social work services; and training to deal with incontinence.

Over half of the rehabilitation agency respondents also cited geriatric assessment and traditional acute care as important components.

Rehabilitation Service Outcomes and Obstacles

Congressional committee respondents described federally funded rehabilitation programs as focusing on employment mainstreaming, improving psychological well-being, maintaining functional ability, maximizing independence, and restoring functional ability. Nearly all rehabilitation agency staff cited employment mainstreaming, and nearly all nonrehabilitation agency respondents cited maintaining functional ability as the primary goal of the rehabilitation-related programs for which they were responsible. Maximizing independence was a secondary goal for all agencies. Although restoring functional ability was a lesser program goal, both congressional and state respondents agreed that it is a necessary and important objective.

While all respondents reported that their programs met the stated program objectives, nearly all described the current mix of federal and state geriatric rehabilitation programs as somewhat or totally inadequate. About three-quarters of all respondents alleged that few public services are currently available because of federal and state budget constraints. Nearly half also suggested that services are lacking because of limited evidence of cost-effectiveness and positive outcomes of rehabilitation for older persons, the feeling that "you can rehabilitate the young but only maintain the old," and the structure of benefits in existing programs. Nearly half of the rehabilitation agency staff also asserted that acute care is still perceived by most policy makers as more important than chronic care.

Aging and Rehabilitation Advocacy

Both congressional and state agency respondents indicated that past lobbying efforts of aging and rehabilitation interest groups have expressed narrow and seldom overlapping concerns. They suggested that interest groups open discussions with each other and broaden their advocacy efforts (e.g., by forming coalitions). The survey respondents also encouraged groups to take more active responsibility for ensuring that existing educational systems adequately train health and social support providers on aging, disability, and rehabilitation issues.

IMPLICATIONS FOR POLICY MAKERS AND SERVICE PROVIDERS

Recent legislative efforts suggest that rehabilitation policies may yet be reformed to accommodate the needs of older as well as younger persons with disabilities. Such efforts increasingly acknowledge the need to shift from the traditional acute care model of health services and work-life model of rehabilitation services to a more flexible long-term-care and active-life model. Also, limited public and private home- and community-based health and support services *do* exist—for persons who can afford them. However, because the services are often quite expensive, many elderly are unable to benefit from them (Rivlin and Wiener, 1988). Recent studies found that older persons who have the greatest numbers of disabilities are disproportionately poor (Smeeding and Straub, 1987; U.S. House of Representatives, 1987; Smeeding, 1990; Families USA, 1990). Our nation's challenge will be to develop and finance rehabilitative services and benefits that are appropriate, adequate, and accessible to all persons with disabilities.

In the meantime, most existing public rehabilitation and long-term-care policies continue to be biased against comprehensive and noninstitutional approaches to providing rehabilitation for people with disabilities. In turn, this bias adversely affects service funding and delivery, the priority given to treating older persons in comparison with serving younger persons with disabilities, and the training of appropriate rehabilitation personnel (Katov, 1990; Kemp et al., 1990).

The congressional and state agency survey findings suggest that *comprehensive* rehabilitation programs for older persons are widely unavailable because few policy makers or providers see them as priority needs. In particular, services that aim to restore function are not yet perceived as "doable and desirable" for older persons as they are for younger persons with disabilities.

Despite policy maker and provider knowledge of disabling conditions and the need for appropriate rehabilitation services, including restorative strategies, flexibility to pay for such services remains limited in existing state- and federally-funded programs. While budget deficits are serious and real constraints in providing rehabilitation services, deficits may be used by policy makers as excuses to mask ageist attitudes that underlie decisions on service delivery to older persons. Inconsistent cost-effectiveness data and limited advocacy for such services also work against a sense of priority and urgency among policy makers.

These findings and the current literature call for a bottom-up approach to the development of policy alternatives to meet future rehabilitation needs: collection of data to support the need for and effectiveness of services; public and provider education on aging, disability, and rehabilitation issues; and grass-roots advocacy by interest groups, consumers, and their families for appropriate services.

First, interdisciplinary research data must be collected on disabling conditions and rehabilitation services. Government should take an active role in sponsoring rigorous research on issues such as the incidence, prevalence, and trajectory of both early- and late-life-onset chronic disabling conditions; the relative costs, effectiveness, benefits, and utilization of medical and nonmedical health and supportive services; the social and economic barriers to perceiving the existence of, adjusting to, and seeking assistance for disabling conditions; and the development and efficacy of assessment and outcome tools.

Second, educators must use these data to properly train health and social-support professionals on rehabilitation issues for both younger *and* older persons with disabilities. Incentives must be offered for professionals to choose geriatric specialties and to participate in multidisciplinary assessments and service delivery. Such incentives might include targeting educational benefits and changing healthcare reimbursement policies to encourage training for both medical and nonmedical rehabilitation strategies.

Finally, grass-roots consumer and provider groups must work with researchers and educators to inform the public about the implications of aging and functional losses and to articulate their concerns and needs to policy makers at federal, state, and local levels. These research, educational, and advocacy strategies are critical to countering public misperceptions about aging, disability, and rehabilitation and to ensuring the development and financing of effective and efficient rehabilitation services for all persons with disabilities.

ACKNOWLEDGMENTS

The authors thank Bryan Kemp, director of the Rancho Los Amigos Rehabilitation Research and Training Center on Aging in Los Angeles County, for his guidance on the Geriatric Rehabilitation Policy Alternatives project, and Debra Sheets for her research assistance and helpful comments on earlier drafts of this article.

* * *

Linda A. Wray is a doctoral candidate, Andrus Gerontology Center, University of Southern California, Los Angeles, and Fernando Torres-Gil, Ph.D., is professor of social welfare, University of California, Los Angeles.

REFERENCES

Anderson, T. P., Baldridge, M. and Ettinger, M. G., 1979. "Quality of Care for Completed Stroke Without Rehabilitation: Evaluating by Assessing Patient Outcomes." *Archives of Physical Rehabilitation* 60:103–7.

Becker, G. and Kaufman, S., 1988. "Old Age, Rehabilitation, and Research: A Review of the Issues." *Gerontologist* 28(4):459–69.

Benedict, R. I. and Ganikos, M. L., 1981. "Coming to Terms with Ageism in Rehabilitation." *Journal of Rehabilitation* 47:10–18.

Binstock, R. H., 1990. "Allocation of Resources to Rehabilitation: Intellectual and Political Challenges." In S. J. Brody and L. G. Pawlson, eds., *Aging and Rehabilitation II: The State of the Practice.* New York: Springer.

Branch, L. G. et al., 1984. "A Prospective Study of Functional Status Among Community Elderly." *American Journal of Public Health* 73: 266–68.

Branch, L. G. and Ku, L., 1989. "Transition Probabilities for the Elderly over a Decade: Uses in Long-Term Care Financing." *Journal of Aging and Health* 1:370–408.

Brody, S. J. and Ruff, G. E. eds., 1986. *Aging and Rehabilitation: Advances in the State of the Art.* New York: Springer.

Brody, S. J. and Pawlson, L. G. eds., 1990. *Aging and Rehabilitation II: The State of the Practice.* New York: Springer.

Crimmins, E. M. and Saito, Y., 1990. "Getting Better and Getting Worse: Transitions in Functional Status Among Older Americans." Paper presented at the Annual Meeting of the Population Association of America, Toronto, Canada, May.

Crimmins, E. M., Saito, Y. and Ingegneri, D., 1989. "Changes in Life Expectancy and Disability-Free Life Expectancy in the United States," *Population and Development Review* 15(2):235–67.

Cromar, E., 1984. "Research and the Disabled Elderly." *Generations* 8(4): 55–58.

Families USA, 1990. *Down Payment on Dignity: Beginning to Meet the Home Care Needs of America's Frail Elderly.* Washington, D.C.: Families USA Foundation.

Frymoyer, J. W., 1986. "Musculoskeletal Disabilities." In S. J. Brody and G. E. Ruff, eds., *Aging and Rehabilitation: Advances in the State of the Art.* New York: Springer.

GAO, 1989. *Long-Term Care for the Elderly: Issues of Need, Access, and Cost.* GAO/HRD-89-4. Washington, D.C.: General Accounting Office.

Granger, C. V., 1986. "Goals of Rehabilitation of the Disabled Elderly: A Conceptual Approach." In S. J. Brody and G. E. Ruff, eds., *Aging and Rehabilitation: Advances in the State of the Art.* New York: Springer.

Johnston, M. V. and Keith, R. A., 1983. "Cost-Benefits of Medical Rehabilitation: Review and Critique." *Archives of Physical Medicine and Rehabilitation* 64:147–53.

Kane, R. L., 1990. "Measuring the Effectiveness of Rehabilitation Programs." In B. Kemp, K. Brummel-Smith and J. W. Ramsdell, eds., *Geriatric Rehabilitation.* Boston, Mass.: College-Hill Press.

Kane, R. A. and Kane, R. L., 1990. *Long-Term Care: Principles, Programs, and Policies.* New York: Springer.

Kane, R. L., Ouslander, J. G. and Abrass, I., 1984. *Essentials of Clinical Geriatrics.* New York: McGraw-Hill.

Katov, C., 1990. *Access to Geriatric Rehabilitation Services: A Background Paper.* Washington, D.C.: American Association of Retired Persons.

Kemp, B., Brummel-Smith, K. and Ramsdell, J. W., eds., 1990. *Geriatric Rehabilitation.* Boston, Mass.: College-Hill Press.

Kovar, M. G. and Feinleib, M., 1991. "Older Americans Present a Double Challenge: Preventing Disability and Providing Care." *American Journal of Public Health* 81(3):287–88.

Leutz, W. et al., 1988. "Targeting Expanded Care to the Aged: Early SHMO Experience." *Gerontologist* 28(1):4–17.

Manton, K. S., 1988. "A Longitudinal Study of Functional Change and Mortality in the United States." *Journal of Gerontology* 43(5):S153–S161.

National Center for Health Statistics, 1987. *Advance Data from Vital and Health Statistics,* No. 133 DHHS Pub. No. (PHS) 87–1250. Hyattsville, Md.: Public Health Service.

Olshansky, S. J. et al., 1991. "Trading Off Longer Life for Worsening Health: The Expansion of Morbidity Hypothesis." *Journal of Aging and Health* 3(2):194–216.

Price, R. J. and O'Shaughnessy, C., 1990. *Long-Term Care for the Elderly.* CRS Issue Brief IB88098. Washington, D.C.: Congressional Research Service, Library of Congress.

Rivlin, A. M. and Wiener, J. M., 1988. *Caring for the Disabled Elderly: Who Will Pay?* Washington, D.C.: The Brookings Institution.

Smeeding, T. M., 1990. "Toward a Knowledge Base for Long-Term Care Finance." *Gerontologist* 30(1):5–6.

Smeeding, T. M. and Straub, L., 1987. "Health Care Financing Among the Elderly: Who Really Pays the Bills?" *Journal of Health Politics, Policy and Law* 12(1, Spring):35–52.

Torres-Gil, F. M. and Rosenquist, L., 1990. "Public Policy and Geriatric Rehabilitation." In B. Kemp, K. Brummel-Smith, and J. W. Ramsdell, eds., *Geriatric Rehabilitation*. Boston, Mass.: College-Hill Press.

U.S. House of Representatives, 1986. *Long-Term Care Services for the Elderly: Background Materials on Financing and Delivery of Long-Term Care Services for the Elderly.* Comm. Print No. 99-EE. Washington, D.C.: Government Printing Office.

U.S. House of Representatives, 1987. *Long-Term Care and Personal Impoverishment: Seven in Ten Elderly Living Alone Are at Risk.* Comm. Pub No. 100-631. Washington, D.C.: Government Printing Office.

U.S. House of Representatives, 1988. *Providing and Financing Long-Term Care for the Elderly.* Comm. Pub No. 100-653. Washington, D.C.: Government Printing Office.

Verbrugge, L. M, 1984. "Longer Life but Worsening Health? Trends in Health and Mortality of Middle-Aged and Older Persons." *Milbank Quarterly* 62(3):475–519.

Verbrugge, L. M., 1989. "Recent, Present, and Future Health of American Adults." *Annual Review of Public Health* 10:333–61.

Verbrugge, L. M., 1991. "Survival Curves, Prevalence Rates, and Dark Matters Therein." *Journal of Aging and Health* 3(2):217–36.

Weissert, W. G., 1985. "Seven Reasons Why It Is So Difficult to Make Community-Based Long-Term Care Cost Effective." *Health Services Research* 20(4):423–33.

Weissert, W. G., 1988. "The Past and Future of Home- and Community-Based Long-Term Care." *Milbank Quarterly* 66(2):309–88.

Wray, L. A., 1991a. *Geriatric Rehabilitation Policy Alternatives: Technical Report on the Survey of Congressional Committee Staff.* Technical report prepared for Rancho Los Amigos Rehabilitation Research and Training Center on Aging. Los Angeles: University of Southern California.

Wray, L. A., 1991b. *Geriatric Rehabilitation Policy Alternatives: Technical Report on the Survey of State Agency Representatives.* Technical report prepared for Rancho Los Amigos Rehabilitation Research and Training Center on Aging. Los Angeles: University of Southern California.

Chapter 7

What Are We Trying to Restore? A Case for Habilitation

Paul A. Raia

At age 71, Franchetta became legally blind. Her case manager enrolled her in an intensive eight-week rehabilitation program designed to teach her all she needed to know to lead an independent life. For Franchetta, the course lasted only three weeks. Because she could not master the braille, the cane travel, the computer with voice synthesizer, the talking book tape player and, of all things, the fencing class, she had dropped out.

When I talked with her, I found that Franchetta was angry—angry that she was forced to learn skills she didn't need, angry that she was not asked what "independent living" meant to her, and angry that the program was geared for younger, vocationally oriented clients. "I learned how to use the telephone and the stove," she told me. "That's all I need for now."

Because more people are living longer, the number of elders with later-life-onset impairments is also increasing markedly. The field of rehabilitation, once driven both philosophically and financially by the goal of restoring individuals to productive employment, is now being challenged by this new, aged constituency. Elders like Franchetta have greater variability in their adjustment potentials, learning styles, emotional reserves, priorities, and goals than did the young World War II veterans for whom the present rehabilitation model was designed. Our charge, therefore, is to listen to Franchetta and design a more "user friendly" system that will give her, and the millions like her, "all I need for now," and possibly more.

THE HABILITATION MODEL: PHILOSOPHICAL DISTINCTIONS

Recognizing that oversimplification can be dangerous, let me nevertheless try to reduce the traditional rehabilitation model to its essential aim: to restore the individual to the highest state of functional independence possible to achieve productive citizenship. Such an objective derives from our Judeo-Christian ethic and provides palatable justification for public expenditures for its accomplishment. The model's emphasis is on "having" abilities and improving function by means of a case-managed system of delivered services.

The habilitation model, by contrast, is fundamentally a disposition—more an attitude about the goals of rehabilitation than a complete model of delivery systems. Following the humanistic theory of Abraham Maslow, it starts with the premise that an innate drive of every person is to maximize potential as a person. Thus, the essential aim of this model of rehabilitation is not to restore the person to what once was, but to enable inner growth in spite of physical, cognitive, or emotional limitations. The primary learning task for the person is to place value on "being" rather than "having," to use Erich Fromm's terminology.

The habilitation model draws on the definitional distinctions first outlined at the World Health Organization Conference in 1980, which divided physical or emotion limitations into three conceptual components: the impairment, the disability, and the handicap.

Impairment relates to the physical dysfunction. Habilitative intervention here involves medical, surgical and pharmacological strategies, for example. The goal is to preserve, restore, or control the physical integrity of the person. Essentially there would be no difference between rehabilitation and habilitation with regard to the intervention here.

Disability refers to functional capabilities. Interventions may involve prosthesis, physical therapy, rehabilitative education, vocational training, low-vision aids, mobility training, and so on. Habilitation would take an approach to disability different from that of either traditional or geriatric rehabilitation. Under rehabilitation the goal is to impart skills that restore function. As a case in point, the 26-Closure rehabilitation method of service delivery would establish a service plan for Franchetta that would have as its goal to restore her to her role as a fully functioning homemaker. Clearly, from the vignette, Franchetta wanted a more limited role. Because of her sight loss, Franchetta was making a choice to be more "dependent" functionally, but not emotionally. Nothing was available to Franchetta within traditional rehabilitation to help her emotional adjustment. Under habilitation the goal is to maximize the emotional growth of the person so that improvement in function is sought only when the person is emotionally ready to learn new skills and only if these new skills lead to emotional adjustment. Individuals can opt for greater dependence and still be emotionally adjusted to their disability. The primary difference here is that rehabilitation seeks control of the external environment, whereas habilitation fosters control of the individual's internal environment. Broad or limited improvements in function may be one way a person chooses to master internal control.

Handicap, the third component, is the executor of the three-part framework. It involves the person's emotional reaction to the condition and how that person defines him- or herself and this new role. This emotional reaction determines, to a large extent, the individual's readiness to participate in the whole process leading to change. Geriatric rehabilitation approaches have overlooked this important point. For example, in a 1988 summary of the 25 projects funded under Title VIIC "Independent Living Services for Older Blind Individuals," only in two projects, Maryland's and Michigan's, was any significant time spent preparing clients emotionally for the task of learning skills, and only Maryland used the habilitation approach, employing individual counseling (by blind psychologists and social workers), family counseling, peer mentors, self-help groups, and social groups before and during any learning of skills.

HABILITATION IN PRACTICE

The habilitative approach can be applied in situations of lifelong and late-life-onset disability with any age group, with any single disability or combination of disabilities, and with any degree of severity of disability. It requires the professional to adopt new attitudes about rehabilitation practice, and the client to assume different responsibilities in the process of change. In a sense, the professional and the client in habilitation enter into a contract that allows the client to set the agenda for personal change, and the system is then required to accept that agenda and facilitate its implementation. I have used this approach quite successfully with elderly blind clients, older clients with mental retardation, and clients with Alzheimer's disease.

Let Franchetta's case illustrate how the model might be put into practice. We would first address Franchetta's impairment by making sure that there were no medical, surgical, or pharmacological interventions that had been overlooked. Since adjustment to her handicap is the core task, much time would be spent with Franchetta in individual, family, and group counseling before a habilitation plan was discussed. Goals of this counseling would be the following: (1) to help her understand that she has choices—even the choice to not participate in counseling; (2) to help her understand that having choices leads to control of things around her and of her own emotions; (3) to help her understand that adjustment starts with her involvement in gaining control of her personal growth; and (4) to help her understand that even significant limitations do not inhibit her development and growth as a person.

Next, Franchetta might choose to participate in a mentoring group composed of two or three elderly blind persons who have participated in the program for some period of time and two or three newcomers. These mentors can be Franchetta's primary resources for habilitation—for whatever, for her, can be.

Only after making the above efforts with Franchetta to address issues related to her handicap would we begin work on her disability. She must tell us what she wants to learn and how she wants to learn it. Because Franchetta at first only wanted to continue to care for her husband, children, and grandchildren, she learned how to use the telephone and the stove. These accomplishments were small gains in function, but they had a synergistic impact on her sense of self as nurturer. Two years later, she came back to the program. She learned other skills, again achieving small functional gains that allowed her in time to become a mentor to other elderly blind persons in the community. At each step in the process, Franchetta was making her own choices as an active comanager in the habilitative process.

The conditions of many disabled persons may degenerate, and their levels of dependence may increase over time. Since the focus of habilitation is not on independence, but rather on personal control over those things that are controllable, disabled persons can continue to grow even as their conditions progress or functions decrease.

To illustrate this point, let me outline how I have adapted habilitation to serve individuals with Alzheimer's disease. For those still in early stages of the disease, we provide patient-led therapy groups where patients come together to discuss their fears, frustrations, and goals. The group also addresses how they have learned to cope with their failing memory, disorientation, and problems with judgment.

While the patients are meeting, their families are meeting separately with trained specialists in Alzheimer's behavior. The families learn ways of structuring the environment to help direct the patient's cognition and improve function. Later, as patients become unable to be self-reflective, they move from the therapy group to an adult day health program, where they are involved in other forms of therapy employed to foster adjustment rather than improve function. These include validation, remotivation, life review, sensory stimulation, cognitive control, resocialization, reminiscence, and expressive arts. Caregivers are taught how to create a home environment that supplies the appropriate amount of stimulation for the individual client so that the client can remain active with assistance. Even when the patients are totally dependent, we work on methods that convey to them that they are safe and loved.

Similarly, as older persons with mental retardation experience decline in their ability to perform activities of daily living, we would first want to determine the source of the decline and try to intervene. If medical intervention were not possible, for example because of an organic dementia, we would discontinue use of operant conditioning schedules and initiate behavior management methods such as sensory cuing, which enable patients to continue to do some tasks with assistance while also preserving their self-esteem.

The habilitation model may also improve the attitude of the rehabilitation professional since the focus is changed from what the person (client) cannot do to who the person is. The person is not defined by his or her dysfunction. These features of the model could improve the professional relationship between the elderly or severely disabled person and the service provider because they offer the provider a goal that is attainable. This, in turn, motivates the provider working with special populations, such as those with mental retardation or Alzheimer's disease.

Habilitation is fundamentally different from other approaches in that it affirms without apology or qualification that one's inner growth is a goal, in and of itself. What we are morally obliged to restore, then, in the increasing number of cases like Franchetta's, is our belief in the value of that affirmation.

* * *

Paul A. Raia, Ph.D., is acting president of the Alzheimer's Association of Eastern Massachusetts, Cambridge, Massachusetts.

Chapter 8

The Kona Adult Day Center: Rehabilitation in Adult DayCare

Karen L. Klemme

One of the more exciting roles a contemporary rehabilitation nurse can play is in the community setting, with adult daycare being a prime example. The philosophy of many adult day centers is to promote and maintain each individual's highest level of functional ability. This philosophy is also a cornerstone of rehabilitation. The term rehabilitation comes from the Latin root word "habilitas," which means "to make able" or "to make fit." Within the healthcare arena, rehabilitation refers to the physical restoration of sick or disabled persons—through therapeutic measures and reeducation—so that they can participate in the activities of a normal life within the limits of their physical disability.

Rehabilitation in the geriatric population is critical to the quality of life and can be just as effective as it is with younger age groups. So often our elderly disabled clients may be discharged from the hospital or rehabilitation setting prematurely, especially following a disabling illness or accident. Furthermore, a physical disability can be devastating to the person's own sense of self-worth as well as to the family unit. Family members may find the adjustment to full-time caregiving overwhelming and in frequent conflict with personal or family commitments. Adult daycare clients and their families are both discovering that adult daycare programs can help because they are community-based and designed to meet the needs of functionally impaired adults through an individual plan of care. Adult daycare is defined as "a structured, comprehensive program that provides a variety of health, social and related support services in a protective setting during any part of a day, but less than 24 hour care. Adult day care assists its participants to remain in the community, thus enabling families and other care givers to continue caring for an impaired member at home" (Webb, 1989).

At the Kona Adult Day Center in Kealakekua, Hawaii, offering nursing and healthcare supervision with an emphasis on rehabilitation was determined to be essential in meeting the needs of the clientele. Currently the population at the center is 55 percent physically disabled and 45 percent cognitively disabled. Physical disabilities include stroke, head injury, Parkinson's disease, spinal cord injury, multiple sclerosis, diabetes, and frailty. Many of the clients with cognitive disabilities have dementia or Alzheimer's disease. The program consists of activities and exercise programs, supervised by the activity coordinator. During the course of the day, the health staff provide for routine toileting, personal care, and bathing. Approximately 25 percent of the clients use wheelchairs for their primary mobility. The remainder use canes or walkers or are independent. Each day two snacks and a hot lunch are provided. Lay staff are apprised of each client's needs and are taught how to assist or supervise each client and how to implement his or her individualized rehabilitation program.

In the planning and program development phases at the center, rehabilitation practices were incorporated into care planning and the activities program. Meetings were planned with the various providers of care in our rural community setting. These included physicians, physical therapists, occupational therapists, and speech therapists. We discussed common concerns about the geriatric client. Some of these were expressed as the need for continuation of home exercise programs and ensuring their incorporation into activities of daily living. At the conclusion of the planning process, a rehabilitation program was developed.

In our active therapy program, we continue the discharge exercise plan carried over from the acute care setting. (The plan is usually developed by a physical therapist in the hospital.) Doing so creates a smooth transition from a highly supervised and structured setting to the home and community setting. Clients with recent strokes are asked to participate in active exercises, including transferring, stair climbing, and walking between parallel bars.

On a typical day the program begins with the clients meeting at the therapy table, with assistance as necessary. Most clients are using wheelchairs, walkers, or canes; many are also using various orthotic devices. The clients begin lying down, with a series of supervised exercises specifically geared for stroke. They are encouraged to count aloud and to participate together as a team. After completion of the active exercises, the clients come to the standing position, using their own walker or quad cane, for example. The next step is to ascend the stairs, practicing methods taught in physical therapy—leading with the stronger side of their body, for example. Last they proceed to the parallel bars, where they practice balance and gait. Clients can use a string of beads to count their own repetitions of each exercise. This technique is particularly useful with aphasic persons and has proven to be a motivational tool whereby clients can monitor their own progress.

The usefulness of this type of program in adult daycare is dramatized by the following case. A client was admitted for daycare after discharge from the local hospital. He had suffered a cardiovascular accident and was left with right hemiparesis. He was 62 years old, aphasic, and used a quad cane, ankle-foot orthosis, and hemisling with resting splint. He was very well known and popular in the community and had been active with his own ranching and farming business. He was very motivated and demonstrated enthusiasm in all he attempted. When he was admitted he required supervision for ambulation, as his balance was poor and unstable. He required assistance in the bathroom with clothing, and he was continent. It was very important for his wife to continue with her work, and she expressed concern since her husband could not remain at home alone.

After one year of daily attendance in the program, he "graduated" and was discharged to his home. He achieved independence in his toileting as he was able to button and zip his blue jeans. He also mastered flushing the toilet with his left hand behind his back. His balance and strength improved to the point where he could walk independently with the use of his quad cane and ankle-foot orthosis. He demonstrated independence by putting on all his own equipment. At home he was able to remove prepared items from the refrigerator, place them in the microwave, and then place them on the table.

This is just one example of how rehabilitation concepts can be applied in the adult daycare setting. Use of these concepts is not limited to the active therapy program; they are also included in activities of daily living and in community outings, which the clients are encouraged to assist the activity coordinator in planning. At the

Kona Adult Day Center, we have seen that a commitment to rehabilitation promotes the individual's capacity to function independently and has a positive impact on the client's self-image and on family dynamics and relationships.

In conclusion, the ultimate goal of rehabilitation in adult daycare is to promote the participant's highest level of independence and functional ability. The geriatric population can achieve the same goals as their younger counterparts although they may require additional time. We need to give them the chance.

* * *

Karen L. Klemme, R.N., B.S.N., C.R.R.N., is nursing coordinator, Kona Adult Day Center, Kealakekua, Hawaii.

REFERENCE

Webb, L., 1989. *Planning and Managing Adult Day Care: Pathways to Success. Owings Mills, Md.:* National Health Publishing.

INDEPENDENT LIVING IN THE COMMUNITY

Chapter 9

Building Coalitions Among Elders, People with Disabilities, and Our Allies*

Julie Ann Racino and Judith E. Heumann

Society is embarking on a new journey. Projections are that more than 20 percent of the population of the United States will be 65 or over by the year 2030 (American Association of Retired Persons, 1990) and that approximately half of this population can be expected to have some limitation in activity resulting from a chronic condition, or what might be called a disability. This situation ushers in a new opportunity to explore common issues faced by people with disabilities and elders and

*This chapter was supported in part by a grant (No. H133B0006-91) awarded to the World Institute on Disability and a cooperative agreement (H133B00003-90) awarded to the Center on Human Policy from the National Institute on Disability and Rehabilitation Research, Office of Special Education and Rehabilitative Services, Department of Education, Washington, DC 20202. The opinions expressed in the chapter are those of the authors, and no official endorsement from the U.S. Department of Education should be inferred.

to learn more from one another about practical strategies that can lead to societal changes enhancing the lifestyles of all of us.

COMMON EXPERIENCES AND SOCIETAL RESPONSES

In December 1989, we assembled a small group in Berkeley, California, to identify areas of common concern among people working actively to change societal responses to elders, people with physical disabilities, and people with mental retardation. Several key societal and service factors (see, e.g., O'Brien, 1989) affect people in all of these groups, particularly individuals who will or might be institutionalized if there is not substantial change in social policy and service practice. These factors include devaluation, "medicalization," regimented care settings, inadequate healthcare, lack of choices, and problems with the service system design.

Devaluation

Over the centuries people of all ages with various disabilities have been perceived as lacking societal worth. Societal devaluation has resulted in people being excluded from the mainstream of their societies, including major areas of community life. Like younger disabled people, older adults—those who are disabled and those who are not—are often seen as being unable to fulfill accepted adult roles (see, e.g., Blaney, 1991). Anyone who becomes defined as a burden, whether because of poverty, age, or disability, faces potential devaluation.

Because of the stigma associated with disability, at least three circumstances commonly arise. Nondisabled people may become more fearful than they ordinarily would be of becoming disabled themselves. People with mild disabilities may be hesitant to associate with people perceived to be more severely disabled. People who have newly acquired disabilities, particularly in the later years, may be fearful of identifying themselves as disabled.

Medicalization

Both the disability and aging fields are dominated by views that interpret disability as a private social trouble requiring medical control and intervention. Social policy reinforces this perspective through the fiscal dominance of such medicalized services as nursing homes, where at least 1.3 million older adults resided in 1985 (American Association of Retired Persons, 1990). While strong critiques of the medical model exist (e.g., Illich, 1976), an older person with a disability may find him- or herself viewed as sick and therefore unable to benefit from technology and supports that could help maintain the person's lifestyle in the community.

Reliance on Institutional, Regimented Care

Both elders and people with disabilities who rely on public support are likely to receive care in institutions, which tend to emphasize group over individual needs and segregate people from the mainstream of society. Most people must exhaust the emotional and financial resources of themselves and their families in trying to obtain in-home services when they are needed.

Despite expressed enthusiasm for in-home support options, states spend very little money on these options for older adults in long-term care and instead primarily invest in institutional and congregate care (Hansen, 1987). Those of us with disabilities who have fought hard in our youth for integration into the mainstream are concerned about being relegated back to these segregated settings when we grow old.

Inadequate Healthcare

In the United States, the availability of healthcare depends upon income, insurability, and physician discretion. People who are poor or who are viewed as "unprofitable" patients also face the public perception that they are seeking charity in trying to obtain decent healthcare. Since "one-fourth of all Americans now experience what people with disabilities have always known—that coverage for health care can be unavailable, unaffordable, or inadequate for times of medical need" (Ohio Developmental Disabilities Planning Council, 1990), the time is politically good for the development of a healthcare system accessible to all citizens.

Lack of Choices

Most people face a pervasive lack of choices when forced to deal with service systems. Services like personal assistance are not viewed as an entitlement and often are controlled by organizations such as healthcare agencies instead of being directed by people obtaining the services.

Both elders and people with disabilities may face the loss of their legal rights because of judgments about competency, for example, or may be placed in positions where they have no choices except confinement at home without adequate supports or life in an institution. People with mental retardation, who, like anyone else, have preferences and desires for a variety of lifestyles, are particularly at risk of being judged incompetent, while greater care and respect seem to characterize approaches to competency issues with elders.

Problems with the Service Design

To a large extent, services for people with disabilities and elders have been organized around the concept of a continuum of services, which is based on the goal of providing the least restrictive environment that is conducive to the person's well-being (e.g., Gelfand, 1988; Hitzing, 1980; Hoggs and Moss, 1990). A common way of representing the continuum is a straight line running from the least restrictive (living at home) to the most restrictive setting (living in a public institution). The most restrictive settings also are the most segregated and offer the most intensive services, while the least restrictive ones are the most integrated, independent, and offer the least intensive services.

In the late 1980s in the field of developmental disabilities, the use of the continuum concept as the guide to service development started to give way to the concept of non-facility-based services (Taylor et al., 1987). As the basis for service design, the continuum concept (Taylor, 1988) is considered flawed because it (1) legitimates the use of restrictive environments such as institutions, (2) erroneously assumes a necessary link between segregation or integration and a particular level of service, (3) supports the primacy of decision making by professionals, (4) sanctions infringements on people's rights, and (5) directs attention to physical settings instead of the supports people need to be integrated into the community.

INDEPENDENT AND SUPPORTIVE LIVING FOR PEOPLE OF ALL AGES

In the 1960s, individuals with disabilities began to organize and create an agenda for action, following the same tenets of other civil rights movements. The independent living movement, controlled by disabled people, has worked to address discrimination and to advocate for the supportive services, such as personal assistance, housing assistance, assistance in finding jobs, and peer support, that are necessary for full participation in the community and society.

One of the most important features of the movement is its goal of self-empowerment. While helping people to recognize that we who are disabled are capable of taking more control over our own lives, the movement has also helped us to learn to respect ourselves as equal human beings.

While younger people with physical disabilities have tended to be most represented in the movement, there is a strong recognition that elders, too, are made powerless because of public ignorance and prejudice. The independent living movement has also made increased efforts to reach out to people with mental retardation and psychiatric disabilities, who meanwhile have formed groups of their own to seek strength from each other and to find their own voices (see, e.g., Williams and Shoultz, 1984; Knight, 1990).

Building on the principles of the independent living movement, people of all ages and abilities are increasingly demanding the right to both a decent home and the supports they want and need (see, e.g., Carling, 1990; Taylor et al., 1987; Zola, 1987). Like those committed to the right to age in place, the independent living and supportive living movements are premised on the value of individual choice and the conviction that people have a right to have intense personal assistance and other necessary services available in their own homes in regular neighborhoods.

THE VISION IN PRACTICE

For both young and old, autonomy and the availability of support services are important to quality of life, and both must have a voice and see that they are heard if systemic change is to occur. Three areas where elders and people with disabilities are coming together in response to common challenges posed in this society are through independent living centers and the national housing and personal assistance agendas.

Independent Living Centers and the Older Adult

Programs called independent living centers began to emerge in the 1970s, primarily in Great Britain, the United States, and Canada (DeJong, 1979). In 1972, the Berkeley Center for Independent Living (CIL) was created by a group of disabled people, some of whom had lived in institutionalized settings and were determined never to return. Internationally, these centers are consumer-controlled organizations combining both policy and services with the goal of increasing the full participation of people with disabilities in society.

The proportion of independent living center participants who are older varies considerably across this country, from a low of approximately 20 percent to a high of 60 to 70 percent at some centers. Although not all centers keep statistics on the ages of the people involved, our experience is that elders are involved in all kinds of center services, including those for people who are blind or visually impaired, accessibility programs, personal assistance referral, equipment loan, and information and referral, among others.

Some independent living centers, such as the Berkeley's CIL, have specifically made efforts to reach out to elders. As early as the 1970s, disabled staff from CIL worked to help disabled elders participate at existing senior centers and to form support groups so that people could benefit from the experiences of others who had faced or were facing similar issues. More recently, the World Institute on Disability (WID) trained older people with disabilities, who were identified at nutrition sites and senior centers, to be peer support trainers. WID assisted disabled elders to become board members at the senior health centers and to run support groups.

The experience of the World Institute on Disability suggests that what elders want is similar to the expressed needs of other people participating in independent living centers. Often, they need basic information about being disabled, about available services, and about technology and other ways to support continued community living and participation. They want opportunities to talk with other people in similar situations.

Housing: Accessible, Affordable, Available

Independent living centers typically do not directly provide housing, but they may be involved with housing referral or accessibility issues. While elders may be facing the prospect of institutionalization for the first time, some people with disabilities, as they become older, are having their first opportunity to live in a regular home in the community (Taylor et al., 1991).

Housing provides a unique focal point for bringing together a range of people to solve common social problems. Some housing organizations, such as the Madison Mutual Housing Association in Wisconsin, are striving to develop mainstream communities that represent as diverse a group of people as possible—people of different generations, mixed incomes, and different household compositions, racial and ethnic backgrounds, and ability levels. To put its value of inclusive communities into practice, this organization turned down federal funding from the Department of Housing and Urban Development's 202 program, which would have segregated people with disabilities, and instead obtained financing from the Wisconsin Power and Light Corporation.

In a recent study of one housing association, Racino (in press) compared issues confronting the integration of the "frail elderly" into a housing cooperative with the integration of people with developmental and physical disabilities. While the "frail elderly" were viewed as needing a "group home" and needing staff to speak on their behalf, people with other disabilities (and apparently greater needs) were living in regular cooperative sites with 24-hour attendant or live-in roommate support. Integration and home living, in this case, appeared to be more a function of how the support organization approached the people it served than a function of the capability levels of the people themselves.

Because of prohibitive and outdated social policies, regulations, and legislation, elders and disabled people may be unable to live in their own homes and still obtain the support services they need. Such "forced choices"—between living at home and receiving needed support—can disrupt people's connections with their neighborhood, friends, and community activities. We must stop erecting buildings, developing programs, and setting policies that divide and segregate elders and people with disabilities from others.

Personal Assistance and Other Support Services

Personal assistance, income supports, technology, and transportation are common solutions that can and are being pursued by elders and people with disabilities (see, e.g., Heumann, 1986). All people need a decent income, and millions of people require some kind of personal assistance, which can be defined as "one person assisting another with tasks that the individual would normally do him or herself if he or she did not have a disability" (Litvak et al., 1991). As one of us described her childhood experiences to the Senate Committee on Labor and Human Resources:

> Then, as now, there were virtually no programs available to pay for assistance. My family and friends were my unpaid providers. . . . In reality, they were never able to meet my needs. I learned early on that I didn't have the right to do things the same way my non-disabled peers did. . . . The help I was getting was voluntary. . . . It meant I shouldn't be too demanding, and I should be thankful for whatever I got. . . . At the age of five, I was denied entrance into school because I needed personal assistance (Heumann, 1991).

Despite the passage of the Americans with Disabilities Act of 1990 (ADA), doors of opportunity will continue to remain closed for the significantly disabled without the creation of a full range of personal assistance services. Together, we are organizing to ensure that personal assistance will be viewed as a civil and human right and available to people of all ages. As one part of the process, disabled people and our allies from 43 states and nine countries met together and unanimously passed a resolution to drive the national personal assistance agenda forward (World Institute on Disability, 1991). Of particular interest to elders are the following aspects, which can form the basis for further joint organizing in this area:

1. Services shall enable users to exercise their rights and to participate in every aspect of sociocultural life, including, but not limited to, home, school, work, cultural and spiritual activities, leisure, travel and political life. . . .
2. These services must be available up to seven days a week, for as many hours as needed, on long-term, short-term and emergency bases. . . .
3. The user should be free to select and/or hire as personal assistants whomever s/he chooses, including family members . . . and
4. Government funding should be an entitlement (WID, 1990).

ACHIEVING CHANGE AND WORKING TOGETHER

The next decade will pose many challenges to people who are concerned about maintaining the right for all people to live and participate in the community. We can no longer afford to be pitted against one another, but must unite around our common interests and expand our efforts at education, advocacy, and research. Steps to achieving these changes include the following:

1. *Develop and maintain a sense of personal empowerment.* Personal empowerment is critical to individual life satisfaction, political organizing, and mutual collaboration. People who are newly disabled should have opportunities to meet people with similar disabilities as well as other role models and potential mentors. Elders, including those with disabilities, must be seen serving on boards of directors, employed on staffs, and included in the development and implementation of programs designed to teach professionals and family members about issues concerning aging. Continued efforts must be made to include and involve elders in independent living centers and in matters concerning disability issues (Heumann, 1986) and to foster concern for aging issues in the disability communities.

2. *Form political coalitions between elders and people with disabilities.* Coalitions of groups of elders and disabled people working in concert with their allies can affect the course of our lives and those of the millions who will become old or disabled in the future. Together, we can fight to ensure that the barriers in U.S. social policy that prohibit decent home living and community life with dignity are addressed. Initial organizing areas include legislation for a national personal assistance program, construction of accessible housing, sufficient funding for assistive technology devices, national health insurance, and prohibition of barriers to home ownership.

3. *Develop strategies to increase networking between the different communities.* Through networking on the local, state, and national levels, we can work toward more valued opportunities in mainstream life for both elders and people with disabilities. Thus, instead of simply integrating adults with disabilities into age-segregated senior services, networking creates opportunities for people to come together and develop strategies for fostering more valued societal roles for all. As one example, training professionals in one another's fields can help to increase exchange and develop the base for greater dialogue.

4. *Debunk the myths of aging and disability through self-examination and media campaigns.* We must commit ourselves to learning from each other. Younger people must learn to become old with dignity and pride, and older people can serve as proud and powerful role models. Elders, people with disabilities, and those who will become older or disabled in the future must work together to overcome our own prejudices and fears about age and disability.

CONCLUSION

The major issues facing people with disabilities today overlap with those confronting the growing population of elders in this country. As critical moral issues like those brought to the fore by right-to-die legislation, are raised, political organizing and education by those who are already subjected to devaluation and "medicalization" has truly become a matter of life and death. Together we can and must meet these challenges. We can afford to do no less and to wait no longer.

* * *

Julie Ann Racino is deputy director, Research and Training Center on Community Integration, Center on Human Policy, Syracuse University, Syracuse, N.Y. Judith E. Heumann is cofounder and vice president, World Institute on Disability, Oakland, California.

AUTHORS' NOTE

In this chapter the authors use both the terms *people with disabilities* and *disabled people,* based on the preferences of the different constituencies the authors represent.

ACKNOWLEDGMENTS

The authors would like to thank Steve Taylor, as well as Nancy Eustis and Ed Ansello, for their comments on an earlier draft of this chapter.

REFERENCES

American Association of Retired Persons, 1990. *A Profile of Older Americans.* Washington, D.C.

Blaney, B., 1991. *Planning Our Vision: A Resource Handbook on Aging and Developmental Disabilities.* Cambridge, Mass.: Human Services Research Institute.

Carling, P., 1990. "Community Integration of People with Psychiatric Disabilities: Emerging Trends." In J. Jacobson, S. Burchard and P. Carling, eds., *Clinical Services, Social Adjustment, and Work Life in Community Living.* Baltimore, Md.: Johns Hopkins University Press.

DeJong, D., 1979. *The Movement for Independence: Origins, Ideology and Implications for Disability Research.* East Lansing: Michigan State University, University Center for Instructional Rehabilitation.

Gelfand, D., 1988. *The Aging Network: Programs and Services (3rd Edition).* New York: Springer.

Hansen, K., 1987. *Long-Term Care for the Elderly.* Denver, Colo.: National Council on State Legislators.

Heumann, J., 1986. "The Independent Living Movement: Benefits for the Elderly." In C. Estes, J. Heumann and C. Mahoney, eds., *Toward a Unified Agenda: Proceedings of a National Conference on Aging and Disability.* San Francisco: Institute on Health and Aging, University of California.

Heumann, J., 1991, Presentation Before the Senate Committee on Labor and Human Resources, Washington, D.C., July 25. Oakland, Calif.: World Institute on Disability.

Hitzing, W., 1980. "ENCOR and Beyond." In T. Apolloni, J. Cappuccilli and T. P. Cooke, eds., *Towards Excellence: Achievements in Residential Services for People with Disabilities.* Baltimore, Md.: University Park Press.

Hoggs, J. and Moss, S., 1990. "Social and Community Integration." In M. P. Janicki and M. M. Seltzer, eds., *Aging and Developmental Disabilities: Challenges for the 1990s (Proceedings of the Boston Roundtable on Research Issues and Applications in Aging and Developmental Disabilities).* Washington, D.C.: Special Interest Group on Aging, American Association on Mental Retardation.

Illich, I., 1976. *Medical Nemesis: The Expropriation of Health.* New York: Random House.

Knight, C., 1990. *Stigma: Stereotypes and Scapegoats.* Columbus, Ohio: Ohio Legal Rights Services.

Litvak, S., Zukas, H. and Brown, S., 1991. "A Brief Economy of Personal Assistance Services." *Spinal Cord Injury Life,* Spring: 3–5.

O'Brien, J., 1989. *Common Interests Among People Concerned with Changing Societal Responses to Elders, People with Physical Disabilities, and People with Cognitive Disabilities.* Summary of a Working Group sponsored by the World Institute on Disability and the Center on Human Policy on December 9, 1989, Berkeley, Calif.

Ohio Developmental Disabilities Planning Council, 1990. *Insuring Health Care for People with Disabilities.* Columbus.

Racino, J. A., in press. "The Madison Mutual Housing Association: People and Housing Building Communities." In J. A. Racino et al., eds., *Housing, Support and Community: Choices and Strategies for Adults with Disabilities.* Baltimore, Md.: Paul H. Brookes.

Taylor, S. J., 1988. "Caught in the Continuum: A Critical Analysis of the Principle of the Least Restrictive Environment." *Journal of the Association of Persons with Severe Handicaps* 13(1):41–53.

Taylor, S. J., Bogdan, R. and Racino, J. A., eds., 1991. *Life in the Community: Case Studies of Organizations Supporting People with Disabilities*. Baltimore, Md.: Paul H. Brookes.

Taylor, S. J. et al., 1987. *The Nonrestrictive Environment: On Community Integration for Persons with the Most Severe Disabilities*. Syracuse, N.Y.: Human Policy Press.

Williams P. and Shoultz, B., 1984. *We Can Speak for Ourselves: Self-Advocacy for Mentally Handicapped People*. Cambridge, Mass.: Brookline Books.

World Institute on Disability, 1991. "Resolution on Personal Assistance Services." Passed by participants in the International Personal Assistance Services Symposium, September/October, Oakland, Calif.

Zola, I., 1987. "Home Health Care for Older Adults with Disabilities." *Aging Network News* 4(6).

Chapter 10

What Is Independence?

Elias S. Cohen

This chapter approaches the question of independence in terms that emerge from the concept of a right to flourish (Cohen, 1987). The right to flourish suggests there are avenues of "independence" that exist even in tiny bytes of time or in what may appear to be inconsequential arenas of choice. The concept incorporates and elaborates upon Collopy's conceptual framework of autonomy (Collopy, 1988). In Collopy's terms, autonomy (in one of its configurations) may be decisional or executional. That is, an individual may be capable of making decisions and giving direction even though carrying out the decision by the individual is impossible. Autonomy may be achieved and maintained by exercising control over agents or equipment to carry out decisions. Furthermore, this chapter uses the sense applied to the term by the independent living movement, which holds that autonomy is infused with the notion of achievement of individual consumer goals (see, for example, Johnson,1987). If autonomy is seen in this light, disability and services must be redefined.

In contrast to the field of aging, the independent living movement views services less as compensating for physical and psychological deficits than as enhancing or limiting independence. Services are examined with an eye to whether they are controlled and directed by the consumer or by the agency. The purposes of services are measured against a standard that accepts risk-taking and uncertainty rather than a standard that concentrates on assured safety, quality, and protection. And finally, services are directed at goals that (1) include involvement and engagement, which give life meaning and (2) go beyond survival and the limited aim of staying out of an institution (Berkowitz, 1987).

Lex Frieden, currently the senior vice president of the Texas Institute for Rehabilitation and Research and formerly chairman of the President's Committee on the Employment of People with Disabilities, illustrates the point about view of self in a short autobiographical vignette he presented at a conference in Philadelphia some years ago. When he left his parents' home after having had an accident in which he suffered a spinal cord injury, his parents drove him to an independent living center so that he could learn to live on his own. When evening came, he sought an attendant to help him get into bed. He wheeled along the hall and came to another disabled chap and asked if somebody could help him get into bed. The other fellow pointed to a man with long hair, wearing blue jeans and a chambray shirt. Lex wheeled over to him and said, "Will you help me go to bed?" The fellow said, "Sure! Where's your room?" and Lex said, "Over there." The man just stood there and didn't do anything. Lex asked, "Would you come with me and help me?" And the fellow accompanied him to the room—and just stood there. "Would you lift me onto the bed?" Lex asked, and the fellow said, "Sure," and he lifted him onto the bed, but he didn't do anything. Lex said, "Would you please put my feet up onto the bed?" and the fellow said, "Sure." Lex thought the fellow was stupid and couldn't understand what was going on. As he later told the story, Lex commented, "I had to ask him to take off my shoes, take off my shirt. I thought, maybe he isn't stupid, maybe he's stoned. But when I was in bed, in my pajamas, I realized that was the first time I had undressed myself since my accident."

What a leap! For me, when I say, "I undress myself," it means I take off my clothes. When Lex Frieden had the insight he describes, he knew he was in control and that the attendant was teaching an important lesson. He was teaching him how to use the language, how to think about active verbs that were no longer relevant in their conventional sense to him in his condition but which he could make relevant and could use because of a point of view of control.

APPLICATIONS TO OLDER PERSONS WITH DISABILITIES

Two threshold questions present themselves: "Are the elderly with disabilities different from younger people with disabilities?" and "Do those differences, if any, explain or rationalize different programmatic and attitudinal approaches?"

Consider first the developmental slope—the inevitable biological and psychological decline confronting the elderly who are disabled. After all, elderly people who have suffered some disability have been brought face to face with their own mortality and, very likely, increasing morbidity. For many, 5 years, perhaps 10, may be all that remain, and it is largely down hill. Is that significantly different from the experience of young people with disabilities? If it is not, then the young who have a shortened life expectancy and who face imminent physical decline should also express the same attitude of despair and ennui. In the absence of definitive survey data, I reviewed my experience of the last seven years with advisory committees composed of young people with disabilities, students in a residential vocational rehabilitation center, advisory committees to the vocational rehabilitation agency for the state of Pennsylvania, and representatives of organizations involved in the independent living movement. That review reminded me of the 28- and 30-year-olds I had worked with. These were young men and women who had wasting diseases and who perhap s could look forward to 10 or at best 15 years of continued life, who faced decreasing vital capacity, and for whom even the effort needed to speak increased weekly. I was reminded not only of their social advocacy for the group they represented but of their personal advocacy to assure full participation in those aspects of life in which they were interested—work, transportation, higher education, living in their own apartments, going to a restaurant, negotiating a sidewalk.

My analysis also led me to consider the impact and nature of the onset disability. Most elders with disabilities have come to late life without disabilities, and it is not until the eighth and ninth decades that they may be struck with the disabling effects of arthritis, osteoporosis, cardiovascular accidents, emphysema, blindness, diabetes, and other ailments. They have lived the greater part of their lives as people with*out* disabilities. The assaults coming late in life are the assaults of old age. Is there some real contrast between their situation and that of those who have congenital disabilities—cerebral palsy, spina bifida, skeletal anomalies, and the like? If anything, those with congenital disabilities, it seemed to me, had a harder struggle, if only because they had had little chance to acquire the assets of supportive social organizations of school, workplace, friends, church, etc., because it was so difficult for them to participate in those associations.

The answers to the threshold questions did not rationalize what I perceive to be the difference between young and old vis-à-vis a view of independence. Elsewhere (e.g., Cohen, 1988), I have explored what Rosalie Rosenfelt (1965) dubbed "The Elderly Mystique." I believe that the elderly mystique is alive and well as we approach the twenty-first century. It has changed to the extent that it is now focused on the elderly disabled. The mystique now holds that *any* disability in old age marks the beginning not only of inevitable decline and an ignominious end, but also the end of mastery. According to this mystique, the elderly who become disabled can no longer travel as they wish, eat what they want, engage in physically demanding activities, or exercise dominion over a work space or group of people. They have no schedules they must keep, and so forth. This is the elderly mystique that many disabled elderly may buy into.

Furthermore, and perhaps even worse, the advocates, policy makers, program planners, and practitioners support and nourish the elderly mystique, utilize and promote the "geriactivist" model for successful aging, and fashion programs for the elderly based upon the incompetence model (Minkler, 1990).

AUTONOMY AND IN-HOME CONSUMER-DIRECTED SERVICES

In 1985 Community Services Systems, Inc., undertook a study of three programs that provided personal attendant care to elderly persons in their own homes in California, Maine, and Pennsylvania (Community Services Systems, 1986). The study involved interviews with 57 severely disabled elderly, 14 personal care attendants serving them, 15 professional social workers or nurses, and 9 program executives. Formal content analysis was conducted of reported decision-making activities and expressed preferences by consumers. Researchers also analyzed attitudes of both consumers and agency staff toward autonomy.

The programs examined were organized on a consumer-based model—that is, the consumers, not the providers, made decisions about scheduling care, the nature of care, the training and direction of the attendant, and the general management of the attendant services, including, in some cases, hiring, firing, and handling the payroll. The attendant care consumer model proceeds on the assumption that people with disabilities who are well versed in their own healthcare needs have the necessary ability and skill to direct and monitor their own personal care.

The study was undertaken to investigate three assumptions. First, we wished to examine the applicability of the consumer model to more conventional in-home services such as homemaker service, chore service, in-home nursing or personal care, physical therapy, etc. Second, the study addressed the traditional assumption that the doctrine of least restrictive alternative is congruent with maximized autonomy—that given the opportunity to remain in (or move into) a living arrangement less restrictive than a nursing home, elders and their service providers would adopt an expansive view of how much the elder could participate in the life of his or her family, neighborhood, and community. Finally, we hypothesized that autonomy in making decisions about the details of personal care was the same as, or was inexorably bound to, autonomy in other domains.

We found some confirmation of our basic assumptions and, to our surprise, some challenges to them. First, it became clear that there are, in fact, many aspects of service direction that *can* be carried over into traditional in-home service programs— for example, scheduling of homemaker or chore services in accordance with consumer preferences, selection of duties for the worker, and even training the worker to carry out tasks congruent with the "style" of the consumer.

Second, with regard to our assumptions about least restrictive environments, the goal of "staying home" and out of a nursing home virtually obliterated other goals of exercising autonomy in broader domains. "Staying home," it turned out, was such an overarching goal that living arrangements that might be more liberating were never considered or suggested to disabled elderly clients by service agencies. For example, moving from a wood-stove-heated shack to assisted living with a transportation component could provide a greater range of choices of activities, greater freedom from life-maintaining activities (like collecting wood for a wood-fired stove), greater freedom in electing activities to engage in, and much greater exercise of dominion over space and time.

Third, we found that even where a pure consumer model is utilized, significantly enhanced autonomy for the elderly does not extend outside of the narrow elements of the service delivery itself.

Unexpectedly, we also learned that shifting the *apparent* locus of control from agency to consumer may actually produce *maleficent* results. A shift from agency to consumer may occur without the transmission of adequate information about the real choices that lie before a consumer. A shift without information may do no more than shift attention away from autonomy and participation in community, neighborhood, and family; may "excuse" service givers from concern about overcoming isolation, disability, or barriers to participation; and may convey to consumers the idea that "the least restrictive alternative" is an end in itself rather than a means for enhancing self-determination and well-being.

Our study revealed little investment by either consumers or providers in the principles of the independent living movement or in the elements of the attendant care service program that permitted and fostered autonomy and control. "Living independently" was equated with avoiding or postponing institutionalization.

DISCUSSION: THE ISSUE OF CASE MANAGEMENT

We also found that although case management staff demonstrated considerable originality in designing service packages and working around family needs and schedules when family was a factor, they were *not* concerned with offering clients the broader-based autonomy that is characteristic of attendant care programs for the younger population. Further, the elderly clients were satisfied with services and were not concerned with the autonomy-enhancing features of the consumer-directed model other than that it allowed them to select their attendant.

The "failure" of case management as we encountered it in this study seems to indicate the pervasiveness of the elderly mystique. However, there are elements in case management that deserve comment in the context of the study described above. Case management is undoubtedly one of the most significant and useful developments in human services in the last half-century. It is grounded in careful screening and assessment, involves clients and caregivers, is goal driven, makes specific plans for specific time periods, is cost conscious, and is subjected to monitoring and evaluation (Schneider, 1988). Deficits are noted and compensatory programs and remedies are prescribed, ordered, applied, and subsequently evaluated. However, our study suggests that little, if any, attention is given to reinforcement of autonomous behavior, increasing control and dominion over the larger areas of life activities and relationships. This seems to be, in part, a function of our concentrating on solving specific problems with clearly measurable outcomes. Independence is not readily measurable and therefore is not considered. In the literature of case management, there is little mention of the constructs of autonomy, independence, and the exercise of mastery, dominion, and control (see e.g., *Generations,* 1988).

NEXT STEPS

Like the feminine mystique, the elderly mystique is self-perpetuating and appears to be what the elderly want. Services for the elderly are arranged by agencies on schedules set by agency personnel, delivered by agency employees or agents carrying out agency-determined services. In fact, many services are circumscribed in terms of purpose—that is, transportation to go to the hospital clinic is legitimate, but transportation to a restaurant to celebrate a grandson's birthday or attend a meeting of the local political organization is probably not. Few programs are specifically designed or oriented around enhancing control, mastery, and dominion. Most are designed and oriented around beneficent purposes serving palpable needs as determined by thoughtful, well-meaning agencies and organizations and acquiesced in by the elderly themselves.

How do we break out of this pattern?

- The aging movement needs to enlist leadership from within and without who can articulate an "independence model" for elderly people with disabilities.
- Care management protocols should be reviewed and reconsidered to determine how we can go beyond "compensatory" program prescription in order to enhance autonomous behaviors.
- Professional training must be modified to expose physicians, nurses, social workers, public administrators, and healthcare administrators to the possibilities of consumer-oriented program models.
- Healthcare, rehabilitation, and social service programmers should systematically explore the similarities and differences between and among young and elderly persons with disabilities in terms of attitudes toward rehabilitation, decision making, program control, and desired activities and roles.
- Educators at all levels—elementary, secondary, postsecondary, and professional—must explore the degree to which curricula and syllabi are appropriately sensitive to issues of disability in old age.

The role of elderly people with disabilities in the American family, neighborhood, church or synagogue, and city or town—and the degree to which our education equips us for disability in late life—must all be explored.

* * *

Elias S. Cohen, M.P.A., J.D., is director of Community Services Systems, Inc., Narbeth, Pennsylvania.

REFERENCES

Berkowitz, E. D., 1987. *Disabled Policy: America's Programs for the Handicapped.* Cambridge, England: Cambridge University Press.

Cohen, E. S., 1987. "History of Services for the Memory Impaired Elderly." In *Innovations in the Care of the Memory Impaired Elderly.* New York: New York State Department of Health, pp. 7–16.

Cohen, E. S., 1988. "The Elderly Mystique: Constraints on the Autonomy of the Elderly with Disabilities." *Gerontologist* 28 (Suppl.) (3):24–31.

Collopy, B., 1988. "Autonomy in Long Term Care: Some Crucial Distinctions." *Gerontologist* 28 (Suppl.) (3): 10–17.

Community Services Systems, 1986. *Final Report: Enhancing the Personal Autonomy of the Elderly in Long Term Care: Applications of Consumer Model Attendant Care Principles to Conventional Long Term Care Programs.* Narbeth, Pa.: CSS.

Generations, Fall 1988 issue, which is devoted to case management (vol. 12, no. 5).

Johnson, M., 1987. "The Movement toward the 90s." *Spinal Network.* Boulder, Colo.: Spinal Network and Sam Maddox, pp. 292–94.

Minkler, M., 1990. "Aging and Disability: Behind and Beyond the Stereotypes." *Journal of Aging Studies* (3).

Rosenfelt, R., 1965. "The Elderly Mystique." *Journal of Social Issues* 21 (3): 37–43.

Schneider, B., 1988. "Care Planning: The Core of Case Management." *Generations,* 12(5):16–18.

Chapter 11

Consumer-Directed Homecare: What Makes It Possible?

Charles P. Sabatino and Simi Litvak

If a primary goal of supportive homecare services is to enhance individual independence and autonomy, then the structure and delivery of service should be fundamentally shaped by this goal and value. Yet in examining delivery systems, policy makers seldom scrutinize, or even identify, those aspects of the legal, regulatory, and administrative environment of homecare that either enhance or diminish goals of consumer choice and control.

This chapter is based upon research in which the authors examined variables that appear to affect the extent of consumer direction possible in supportive homecare or personal assistance service programs. Sabatino (1990a) of the American Bar Association's Commission on Legal Problems of the Elderly visited six state homecare supportive service programs that purported to offer a high degree of consumer choice and control over in-home supportive services.[1]

[1] The programs surveyed were (1) the California In-Home Supportive Services program, a large state and Social Services Block Grant-funded program; (2) the Colorado Home Care Allowance program, a state cash supplement received by SSI recipients needing in-home services; (3) the Maine Home Based Care program and the Medicaid waiver-funded program for home and community-based care; (4) the Oklahoma Non-Technical Medical Care program, funded under the regular Medicaid personal care option; (5) the Oregon Medicaid Home and Community-Based Services Waiver and the purely state-funded Oregon Project Independence; and (6) the Wisconsin Community Options Program a state-funded, county-managed program providing in-home supportive services to all age groups.

Litvak, at the World Institute on Disability (WID), conducted a national telephone interview survey of administrators of 157 personal assistance service programs in 1985 and a follow-up written survey of these programs and others in 1989 (Litvak et al., 1987; Litvak and Kennedy, 1990a, 1990b, 1991). WID also developed case studies based on long open-ended interviews with 16 program administrators representing the largest programs in all the funding sources (Litvak et al., 1990). In addition, Litvak conducted site visits to six states providing personal assistance services as part of their regular Medicaid program (Litvak and Kennedy, 1991; Kennedy and Litvak, 1991).

While the specific methodologies and terminology differed, both the American Bar Association (ABA) and WID studies essentially examined four basic questions—the first two focusing on structural issues, and the last two on process issues:

1. What are the system's limitations on who can be a provider?
2. What are the system's limitations on what services can be provided (and paid for)?
3. What is the consumer's role in initially determining a service plan?
4. What is the consumer's role in the ongoing management of services?[2]

Within this framework, several specific factors stand out as key to consumer direction in these programs. For purposes of consistency, the term personal assistance services, or PAS, will be used to refer to the supportive homecare services examined by these studies.[3]

[2] One aspect of PAS programs significantly affecting the amount of user control, but not included in this discussion, is the question of funding and resource allocation. If one cannot get the full amount of services one needs, during the hours one wants, for the activities one prefers, because program resources are inadequate to allow such latitude, the user lacks control over his or her daily life. Discussions of these and other user control issues can be found in the referenced material to this article.

[3] Personal assistance may involve assistance with any tasks individuals would normally do themselves if they did not have a disability. Included are (1) personal maintenance and hygiene tasks such as dressing, bathing, and catheter care; (2) mobility tasks such as getting into and out of bed and wheelchair; (3) household tasks including everything from cooking and cleaning to child rearing; (4) cognitive tasks including money handling and planning; (5) communication tasks such as interpreting and reading.

SYSTEM LIMITATIONS ON WHO CAN PROVIDE CARE

Choice Among Provider Modes

Over 40 percent of PAS programs use more than one of the following provider types: *independent provider* (consumer- or self-employed), *agency provider* (employed by a homecare agency), *public employee* (either civil servant or contract worker) (Litvak and Kennedy, 1991). This does not mean, however, that consumers in these programs were able to choose which type of provider they preferred. Indeed, the ABA study found that the program almost always makes that choice. As of 1988, three-quarters of all PAS programs in the United States used agency providers, about half used independent providers, and one-quarter used government employees. Of these options, the independent provider mode offers the greatest potential for consumer direction. However, it also bears the greatest potential for risk to quality of service if the system does not provide sufficient support to the users, since the latter are thus placed in the role of employer.[4]

Impediments to Using Independent Providers (IPs)

WID research has shown that, when PAS program budgets are compared, independent provider programs have the lowest per-unit cost and provide a higher number of PAS hours per user. The main concern state officials have regarding independent providers is that state or local governments will assume "employer" status over individual providers. The fear is expressed in this way: "We can't get too involved or we might be liable for something." Yet, the meaning of being liable for something is not well understood. Several administrators made it clear that their real concern is that states might be required to pay civil service wages, thereby raising the cost of these bare-bones independent provider model programs. Frequently, fear of tort liability is raised, yet none of the states has had any significant history of litigation in which the program was subjected to tort liability for injury or damages. Indeed, Kapp (1990) suggests that legal liability fears are exaggerated and beyond realistic foundation.

[4] One should not assume that, in contrast to independent providers, agency-provided PAS is risk-free. Findings of a recent focus group and individual interview study on quality conducted by WID (Davis et al., 1992) suggest that agency providers can be unreliable, unresponsive, and unproductive.

Paying Family Providers

Five of the six states surveyed by Sabatino allowed—and even encouraged—family members, variously defined, to become paid providers under certain conditions. This finding is consistent with the findings of Linsk et al. (in press) that 35 states (plus the District of Columbia and Puerto Rico) permit some form of financial payment of relatives for the provision of personal assistance. The 1989 WID survey found that 26 percent of PAS programs allowed family members to become paid providers in some circumstances.

Federal regulations provide that "personal care" services in a recipient's home shall be provided by an individual who is not a member of the recipient's family.[5] However, the term "family" is not defined in the federal regulations and, consequently, states have taken differing views on the scope of "family." Definitions range from long lists of persons related by blood or marriage to only spouses and dependent children. PAS programs with maximum provider choice define the family disqualification as narrowly as possible.

Worker Pay and Benefits

Worker benefits hovered at or slightly above minimum wage in all the programs surveyed in the ABA study. The WID survey found that attendant wages vary by provider type and funding source. Overall, family providers ($4.05) and independent providers (average $4.85) received the lowest hourly wage, and home health ($6.95) and homecare agency workers ($6.62) received the highest wage. Government provider wages were in the $5–$6 range. The WID data indicate that independent providers usually receive only one benefit, mainly Social Security, whereas agency and government providers receive an average of three benefits, usually Social Security, workers' compensation, and unemployment benefits.

Other Work Force Supports

The quantity and quality of the provider work force is a persistent issue nationally, regardless of the provider mode. In the six-program sample, worker shortages were variable within and across the programs and showed no consistent pattern.

[5] 42 C.F.R. §440.170(f)(3).

Administrators consistently noted a need for developing hiring pools more systematically. In addition to providing better wages and benefits, recommendations included recruiting and screening potential workers and providing orientation and training to workers who would be assisting clients unable to train workers on their own.

There appears to be a growing realization among administrators and a conviction among recipients that greater attention to the economic, social, and career needs of the independent provider work force is a prerequisite to ensuring both availability and quality.

SYSTEM LIMITATIONS ON SERVICE PROVISION

The Menu of Services

Most personal assistance programs use the traditional regulatory approach of itemizing a defined set of covered services in the program's regulations. All focus on providing help with activities of daily living as their primary service. Most programs also offer assistance with light housework and meal preparation tasks. Far fewer allow assistance with "paramedical tasks," chores, repairs, excursions outside the home, and communication tasks. In practice, independent provider model programs appear to be somewhat elastic in this regard. Personal assistance service users and their independently hired providers often strike independent agreements on what the provider will and will not do. These "agreements" may occur with agency providers as well.

Nurse Practice Acts

Most state nurse practice acts typically prohibit paid unlicensed individuals from performing nursing functions, such as injections, catheter assistance, or administration of medications. It is not uncommon, however, for PAS workers to assume various quasi "nursing" functions anyway, even though the client's service plan and record will not reflect this.

The California In-Home Supportive Services program (IHSS), the largest and one of the oldest programs in the country, allows the performance of "paramedical" tasks by any person as long as a physician orders it and the person does not "in any way assume to practice as a professional, registered, graduate or trained nurse."[6] The

[6] CAL [Bus. & Prof.] CODE §2727(e).

Massachusetts Personal Care Attendant program trains the users of the service to be able to monitor the quality of their own services, including their health status, and assists clients in training their own attendants in all their personal assistance needs, including paramedical ones.

Texas, Oregon, and Kansas have also modified their nurse practice act to allow for physician oversight of personal attendants performing paramedical tasks, or to emphasize the teaching and supervising function of nurses with respect to unlicensed care providers. Regulations and standards for delegation of medical/nursing functions allow more practical utilization of PAS workers, and arguably safer utilization, since training and supervision can be more realistically addressed instead of ignored.

CONSUMER'S ROLE IN DETERMINING THE INITIAL SERVICE PLAN

Explicit Goals and Philosophy

A well-articulated philosophy of client-control emphasizing flexibility and responsiveness to client preference seems to make a tangible difference to the "culture" and experience of a program. Homecare programs for the elderly have been reluctant to embrace a philosophy of client-control with real bite. To be effective, such a philosophy needs to be iterated and reiterated at all levels of staffing and procedure. A notable example in this regard is Wisconsin's Community Options Program (COP). One goal of the program, according to state regulations, is to give "increased attention to COP participant views, provide greater respect for participant preferences, and value participant choice of providers as well as services."[7] The Wisconsin program requires that consumer "preferences" be documented in the client assessment and case plan.

Two procedural indicators of client-direction particularly relevant to the initial care planning process are (1) active use of client *statement of rights,* and (2) use of some form of *contractual agreement* between client and provider as a formal instrument of the case planning process.

[7] Bureau of Long Term Support, Division of Community Services, Wisconsin Department of health & Social Services (1988). *Community Options Program: Guidelines and Procedures,* §1.01.

Providing a statement of client rights is a far simpler task than implementing them in the daily provision of services (Sabatino, 1990b). Nevertheless, a statement can serve as a useful teaching tool and standard for both providers and consumers.

With respect to client/provider contracts, none of the states in Sabatino's study required such an agreement on a statewide basis. Recipient/provider contracts are commonly advocated by independent living centers for disabled persons, but their potential value and applicability to all consumer-directed PAS models is substantial. If the PAS user is to be central to the service planning process, then the service plan (i.e., agreement) ought to reflect the outcome of decisions made primarily between the client and the provider and embodied in a client/provider agreement.

Gatekeepers

Regardless of program structure, rules, or procedures, a case manager is often the avenue of service access for many homecare consumers. The case manager can be an enhancement or obstacle to consumer empowerment, depending on the assigned responsibilities of the case manager as well as his or her individual beliefs, biases, and skills. Yet, few programs deal adequately with these issues. Typically, agency staff responsible for client assessment, case planning, and case management are forced to balance conflicting mandates—program gatekeeper, on the one hand, and client advocate, on the other. Guidance for resolving such conflicts, for example, in training and minimum qualifications for case managers, may be lacking. In addition, once accepted into a program, many clients may function very well with minimum case management, as discussed in the following paragraphs.

Client Capacity to Manage Services

Assessment of the client's ability and interest in managing his or her own service plan is almost universally ignored in the formal case-assessment process. To the extent that any such assessment occurs, it remains mostly an unarticulated, mysterious function of case managers. Activities of daily living and instrumental activities of daily living have become household concepts in long-term care, but a scale for "activities of service management" is still a foreign notion. The outcome of such an assessment would be a service plan allocating case management responsibilities between the client and the program's case management staff. For clients who are able to and want to take responsibility for all or some management aspects of their PAS, the process could result in a designation of those responsibilities (e.g., responsibility for finding, hiring, training, or supervising one's own PAS workers). For recipients who have significant cognitive or psychiatric disabilities, the process should result in some designation of a surrogate service manager.

To the extent that this kind of assessment and allocation of decision-making responsibility becomes a conscious and deliberate process, it also has the benefit of ensuring a proportionate allocation of responsibility for any risks involved in service delivery. Recipient choice carries with it the possibility that recipients will reject safety in favor of other personal values or desires. In the normal course, a PAS user who deliberately chooses to assume a risk cannot thereafter hold the agency or provider responsible for injury resulting from that risk. A service management assessment and mutual agreement would provide a vehicle conducive both to empowering the recipient and protecting the public program from potential tort liability for injuries resulting from the exercise of recipient choice.

CONSUMER'S ROLE IN ONGOING SERVICE MANAGEMENT

Client Training in Management

A prerequisite of the self-management described in the preceding section is the need to offer training for clients in the management of their services. The importance of training PAS recipients is emphasized in the independent living movement, but few PAS programs offer this as part of their service package and few independent living centers (ILCs) have continuous training available. Virtually no PAS programs for older persons provide recipient training.

Training needs to include not only the mechanics of supervising and managing providers, but also an understanding of the range of service options available, communication and negotiation skills, how to exercise one's rights, what to do if problems or emergencies arise, and how to evaluate providers. Disabled student programs and ILCs have produced training programs, videos, books, and manuals covering these topics. The independent living peer counseling models of training, in both group and individual sessions, have been used successfully in a WID pilot project through senior centers in California's Bay Area and in other ILC training projects.

Though it is true that programs have persistently underestimated clients' ability to manage their own PAS, it would be erroneous to make the opposite assumption that all PAS users can and want to be their own complete service manager. People need to be able to choose from a menu of management services.

Control Over Payroll

The most tangible business aspect of managing independent PAS providers is the payroll function. The power and the authority bestowed by the act of paying providers is sometimes considered *the* benchmark of client empowerment. However, the significance of this function depends upon the individual's values and abilities. Even when capable, some clients view payroll tasks as a headache.

A useful middle ground, recognized by the Internal Revenue Service, is the "fiscal agent" option. Under this approach, the consumer is considered the employer of the independent provider, but the public agency, or an accounting firm, ILC, or other agency handles the payroll function as the consumer's fiscal agent. Several programs use this approach for some or all of their recipients.

Service Monitoring and Backup

A common refrain in discussions about consumer empowerment obstacles is the circumstantial coercion caused by the lack of options when a caregiver gives less than good service. Case managers and recipients readily acknowledge that many people are reluctant to bite the hands they depend upon for day-to-day help, because finding a replacement is so difficult. Most of the programs examined offered little assurance in the way of emergency backup when independent providers fail to appear.

Traditionally, program oversight is done "from above" using a variety of methods ranging from paper reviews of agency performance to periodic telephone contacts with clients or home visits by a case manager. Minimum frequency requirements for these reviews range from one month to one year. None of these methods are particularly effective at monitoring day-to-day activity in the privacy of an individual's home.

Monitoring "from below" by the recipients of the service or their families is much more compatible with recipient empowerment and is effective where it operates under the proper circumstances. First, training the recipients to monitor and evaluate the service is essential. Recipients need to know what is a good quality service and how to get their complaints addressed. Second, they need a mechanism for responding to problems effectively. The process should encourage recipients to speak up and assure them of case management support when they do. Above all, case managers should respond to what recipients say. More formal complaint mechanisms are not especially visible in PAS programs, although they do exist. Systems for identifying and tracking complaints and compiling data on them rarely are in place.

Recipient-oriented monitoring is also enhanced by direct contact between state quality assurance personnel and recipients, or at least a sample of recipients. Formal recipient evaluations of services, including satisfaction measures, offer opportunities for homecare regulators interested in client empowerment. Nosek (1982) has developed one example of a client satisfaction measure that could prove useful in this area.

CONCLUSION

The factors described above do not necessarily carry equal weight in their impact on client direction. Nor is the impact of any one factor consistent, since any number of circumstantial and operational variables may affect the manner in which they influence consumer control over services. However, the framework suggested here is intended to drive home a fundamental point about consumer autonomy in homecare for disabled clients of all ages—namely, that consumer choice and control can become a reality only if the structure and process of delivery systems are built from the ground up on this premise. Imposing a right of consumer choice on a system after the fact will ultimately not succeed, for the controlling parameters will already be entrenched in a traditional provider-controlled mode.

* * *

Charles P. Sabatino, J.D., is assistant director, American Bar Association's Commission on Legal Problems of the Elderly, Washington, D.C. Simi Litvak, Ph.D., O.T.R. is research director, World Institute on Disability and Research and Training Center on Public Policy in Independent Living, Oakland, California.

REFERENCES

Davis, C. A. et al., 1992. "Views of Consumers of All Ages Regarding Quality in Personal Assistance Services." Oakland, Calif.: World Institute on Disability.

Kapp, M. B., 1990. "Improving Choices Regarding Home Care Services: Legal Impediments and Empowerments." *St. Louis University Public Law Review* 10(2).

Kennedy, J. and Litvak, S., 1991. *Case Studies of Six State Personal Assistance Service Programs Funded by the Medicaid Personal Care Option*. Oakland, Calif.: World Institute on Disability.

Linsk, N. et al., in press. *Wages for Caring:Compensating Family Care of the Elderly*. New York: Praeger.

Litvak, S. and Kennedy, J., 1990a. "Chartbook of Tables from FY1988 Personal Assistance Program Survey Data." Appendix B in *New Models for the Provision of Personal Assistance Services*. Oakland, Calif.: World Institute on Disability.

Litvak, S. and Kennedy, J. 1990b. "The Effect of Government Funding Source on Personal Assistance Programs: A Summary of FY1984 Survey Data." Appendix A in *New Models for the Provision of Personal Assistance Services*. Oakland, Calif.: World Institute on Disability.

Litvak, S. and Kennedy, J., 1991. *Policy Issues and Questions Affecting the Medicaid Personal Care Services Optional Benefit*. Oakland, Calif.: World Institute on Disability.

Litvak, S., Heumann, J. and Zukas, H., 1987. *Attending to America: Personal Assistance for Independent Living*. Berkeley, Calif.: World Institute on Disability.

Litvak et al., 1990. "Source Book of Case Study Information." Appendix C in *New Models for the Provision of Personal Assistance Services*. Oakland, Calif.: World Institute on Disability.

Nosek, M. A. and Fuhrer, M. J., 1982. Development of an Instrument to Measure Adequacy of Personal Assistance Services. *Journal of Rehabilitation Research and Development*. Supplement.

Sabatino, C., 1990a. *Lessons for Enhancing Consumer-Directed Approaches in Home Care*. Washington, D.C.: American Bar Association.

Sabatino, C., 1990b. "Client-Rights Regulations and the Autonomy of Homecare Consumers." *Generations* 14 (Supplement):21-24.

Chapter 12

Adjusting to Early- and Late-Onset Disability: A Personal Perspective

Jean B. Zink

I met Bill at the Kennedy Center on a tour especially designed for people who use wheelchairs. I had made plans to take this tour, but Bill, visiting from California, just happened upon it.

Bill engaged me in conversation throughout the tour. After, while the others discussed the Kennedy Center, all of our discussion revolved around disability. It is not unusual for able-bodied strangers to engage me in conversation about disability, almost always telling me of someone they know who has a disability similar to mine, but it is unusual for people who are disabled to be so direct.

I am fascinated by the lives of disabled people. I wonder how they became disabled and what their lives are like and how their perceptions compare to mine. I was especially interested in Bill because he appeared to be about my age—mid-50s—with a similar disability.

The immediate and observable difference between Bill and me was that Bill was laboriously propelling his own wheelchair. I was accepting help in difficult spots over rugs and up ramps. For me, conserving my energy is paramount. For Bill, accepting no help is essential—a very common response for newly disabled people.

Bill's paraplegia is the result of a construction accident that occurred about six years ago. Usually this type of injury is static, but he says that he continues to deteriorate. Age, he says, is not a factor.

As a young man, Bill freed himself of the responsibility of wife and children. He became a free spirit, working at different jobs and roaming the beaches of California searching for adventure—mostly in the form of short-term relationships. He owns a beautiful but wheelchair-inaccessible home on the ocean. Bill prefers crawling up and down stairs to any type of equipment that may make his home look like the home of a "cripple."

Just after my 16th birthday I contracted polio, which completely paralyzed me. With intensive therapy and lots of good luck, I regained the use of my upper body, with some residual weakness. I married at 21, had a daughter, and was a homemaker until I started working part time seven years ago. My home is handicapped-accessible.

As I listened to Bill talk about his accident and the resulting disability, I realized that this disability was alien to him. He did not intend to become a person who considered disability a part of himself. He also felt that there was nothing in his life that was now normal. This contrasts sharply with my early training, which suggested that being disabled is a normal way of life. I questioned this at the time and still feel unsure, but I came to have as my goal the normalization of my life.

It was as Bill and I talked about this that I realized that the age when one becomes disabled plays such a significant part in how one accepts it. I have long been aware of differences in perception between people who were born with a disability and those, like me, who were briefly socialized in the able-bodied community before becoming disabled. While talking to Bill, I began to consider, as well, the difference between people like me, disabled early in life, and people like Bill, who become disabled late in life after having lived most of their adult lives in the able-bodied community.

We both know what it means to be disabled and to be able-bodied, but the lived experience is extremely different. The role that psychic energy, which is the glory of youth, plays in the process of adjusting to a disability is one example. Without a tremendous amount of disciplined psychic energy, it is impossible for a person with a disability to live in the mainstream, and it is difficult to summon this energy as one grows older. It is difficult to make the changes in self-perception and social status and adapt to the changes in the ordinary tasks of each day. As I meet new demands on my body—postpolio syndrome, for example—I find that I must search for the psychic energy to do so and get on with life. It occurred to me that Bill was having the same difficulty with the new and unusual demands on his body.

Disability came to Bill in his mature life, which was full of fun and freedom, and he feels he was robbed of it. Bill's future is now in the past. Disability robbed me of a carefree youth but not of youth itself, which was full of innocence and idealism. My future was before me. Bill yearns for the past, I prayed for a future. I was 16, and my personality was developing. I was looking to the future, believing I could make a life for myself, if only given the chance. I did not have a past to long for. Part of youth is a belief in the unending future.

Bill asked me the question that is often posed by able-bodied people: How could you possibly spend 40 years using a wheelchair and still want to live? I am always at a loss to answer that question because buried in it, in some unconscious way, is the suggestion that life must not have been worth living. I was at a double loss to answer Bill, who was probably, on a day-to-day level, quite used to his disability but who expressed to my able-bodied companion and me the perception that this life is not worth living.

I did not respond to Bill, because I do not have an answer that makes sense to an able-bodied person, much less to a person who is himself disabled. I struggle every day, as Bill does, but I realize the profound effect disability has had on my life, my thoughts, my relationships. All that I have experienced in my adult life of love and laughter, sadness and despair, anticipation and disappointment has been lived with a disability. Disability is like a filter through which my life has flowed. If by some miracle, I became able-bodied today, the world of the able-bodied would be as alien to me as the world of disability is to Bill.

Most of Bill's life experiences have been lived with strength, energy, and freedom as givens. But Bill lost the life that was precious to him, and now he ages with regret. I age with gratitude, regardless of the struggle, not because I am better than Bill but because my experience as I perceive it has demanded this of me. Bill seems to believe that the way things *were* should be pursued relentlessly. Bill uses his psychic energy to recapture the past. I use my psychic energy to maintain the present.

Freedom was Bill's life, both physically and psychologically. He cannot imagine being hemmed in by his lack of strength. My self-image is intimately bound to my disability. Bill's self-image is locked firmly in the able-bodied world. I share with Bill the dread of increased disability with aging, but age itself is a kind of triumph for me because I have survived.

I think the difference between Bill and me is the difference between life-long disability (and the discipline it demands) and late-life disability. While it is necessary for me to focus my life in a different way and normalize the abnormal, Bill may not need to do this at all. He has lived another life and has a clear idea of the good life. Bill's ideas are for him life giving and life focusing. He doesn't need the cerebral dogmas that fashion my life. His determination, his energy, his love of life are making it possible for him to carry on. I do not think his personality will ever be modified to the extent that mine has been just because, no matter how long his struggle, he had another life.

Disability advocates torture the English language by insisting that people should never be referred to as "disabled persons" but rather as "persons with a disability." I think the distinction is useful within the disabled community. However, I believe that I *am* a *disabled person*, so tempered is my life by the year-in and year-out demands of this disability on me and my family. Perhaps Bill (and others with late-onset disabilities) is a *person with a disability*. He had, and still has, a self that is separate from his disability.

In our declining years, Bill and I may come to share some of the same perceptions. I may be less buoyed by my survival as it becomes even more difficult. Bill may be less determined to appear able-bodied and may install a few ramps and chair lifts in his split-level house. We may both mellow or become very tired of it all. But, whatever paths our lives take or however much age invades the lives we have made, the process of Bill's adjustment to life with a disability will be vastly different from mine.

* * *

Jean B. Zink is a faculty research assistant at the University of Maryland Center on Aging, College Park, Maryland.

Chapter 13

Planning for the Transfer of Care*

Joan B. Wood and Laura Lopater Skiles

Most individuals with lifelong disabilities live with their families, who provide care for them, often throughout their entire lives. Non-family placement of adults with disabilities, in a residential facility, for example, often does not take place until death or disability of the family caregiver occurs.

In earlier times, indeed until the last few decades, life expectancy of individuals with developmental or lifelong disabilities was shorter than that of the population in general. Parents did not expect children with disabilities to survive beyond young adulthood. However, recent demographic trends toward increased longevity among the general population can also be observed among persons with disabilities, and parents of a child with disabilities are now likely to be survived by that child.

As a result of these increases in life expectancy, the period of family caregiving for a relative with a disability has also been prolonged. The two-generation geriatric household is not uncommon. In these situations, parents in their 70s, 80s or even 90s are caring for an adult child with a disability who may also be considered elderly. The parent

*This project was funded by a Developmental Disabilities Basic State Grant to the Virginia Department for the Aging from the Board for Rights of Virginians with Disabilities, which is the Developmental Disabilities Planning Council for the Commonwealth of Virginia. Results were reported in a presentation at the Annual Scientific Meeting of the Gerontological Society of America, San Francisco, Calif., November, 1991.

caregivers, who are dealing with the stresses of their own aging, are often more frail than the younger person with a lifelong disability for whom they are caring.

Studies (Carswell and Hartig, 1979; Heller and Factor, 1991; Roberto, 1988; Turnbull et al., 1986) indicate that many of these caregivers have not made plans for the transfer of care. Long-term planning would include residential, legal, and financial arrangements that would be activated at some specified future time (Seltzer and Seltzer, 1985) and, presumably, could also include psychological preparation of both caregiver and care receiver for a time when the caregiver may no longer be able to provide care.

Recently the authors interviewed 44 family caregivers (ages 55 and older) of persons with developmental disabilities. Most caregivers indicated that they had taken some steps to plan for permanent care of the dependent family member. These steps included making a will (65 percent), contacting a lawyer to discuss estate planning (47 percent), investigating guardianship procedures (29 percent), meeting with care provider agencies (38 percent), or touring residential facilities (29 percent). These percentages also indicate that substantial numbers of families in this sample have not made adequate plans for the transfer of care.

Eighty-four percent of the caregivers indicated that they had made financial arrangements to provide for care of the relative with a developmental disability. These arrangements include savings accounts (23 percent), trust funds (19 percent), life insurance benefits (10 percent), and investments in property (5 percent). In most instances, however, the financial "plans" consisted only of the hope that Social Security benefits would be adequate to provide care for the dependent family member.

Some family caregivers had made no plans other than to arrange with another family member to provide care. Sixty-one percent reported anticipating that another family member or close family friend would provide care when the current family caregiver is no longer able to do so. In many instances, arrangements to accomplish the transfer had not been made and frequently had not even been discussed. Thirty-seven percent, or 16 of the 44 caregivers interviewed, indicated that they do not know who will provide care when they are unable to do so.

Most caregivers clearly did not expect to be survived by the persons for whom they were providing care. They also seemed unable to express their feelings regarding this issue. Some discussed examples of deteriorating health or the increase in one or more chronic health conditions in the adult child with the disability. Caregivers shared their concerns regarding the increase in visits to physicians for medical procedures or medication adjustments. Very few of the aforementioned 61 percent of caregivers who believe that another family member will take over caregiving responsibilities have revised their wills to reflect the identification of the new caregiver or the financial adjustments that must be made to ensure the transfer of care. A few parents openly admitted that if they had their choice they wanted their adult child "to die the breath before I do," thereby relieving other family members of the responsibility of caring for the adult child with a disability and also relieving the caregiver of the need to make extensive plans for the transfer of care.

Whatever the plans, 70 percent of the family caregivers had *not* discussed them with the family members for whom they were providing care. If financial and residential plans have not been discussed, it seems fair to assume that no emotional or psychological preparation has been made for the possibility of the caregiver's eventual death or potential inability to continue providing care. Other data from this study showed that many of the care recipients did not attend funerals or participate in other related activities when a family member died. This suggests difficulty in dealing with death or infantilization of the family member with the disability.

The findings of this study are consistent with those of Heller and Factor (1991) and Roberto (1988), who also found that substantial numbers of families have not made adequate plans for transfer of care. A number of explanatory factors may be involved. First, many current older cohorts of individuals with lifelong disabilities experienced the stigma associated with being considered "handicapped" and had limited opportunities for participation in activities outside the realm of home and family. For this reason, their caregivers may be overprotective and may experience a good deal of ambivalence about the prospect of transferring care.

Second, mutual dependencies between caregiver and care receiver may have developed. Continued involvement with the adult child may be a source of important emotional and psychological benefit (Seltzer et al., 1991), which the caregiver is reluctant to give up. The caregiving role may be a source of identity and ego satisfaction, especially for the female caregiver.

A third factor in failure to plan for the transfer of care may be found in caregivers' appraisal of acceptable alternatives for care, which may reflect limited awareness of the availability of services or actual gaps in available services.

In any case, service delivery agencies increasingly report the "Friday afternoon phone call." In this scenario, the formal service provider receives a frantic telephone call from a relative seeking emergency residential placement for an individual with one or more disabilities because the family caregiver has died or is seriously ill. The service provider is at a disadvantage in this kind of crisis atmosphere, and families may face few available options. Often the individual is given a temporary placement while suitable arrangements are explored. This may be traumatizing for the person with a lifelong disability who has received sheltered care from family members and who now has little opportunity to prepare for a transition.

Heller and Factor (1991) found that information about use of formal services (e.g., respite, case management) increased the probability that caregivers would prefer a residential program placement. Perhaps familiarity with support services for family caregivers can serve to decrease apprehensiveness about formal services and facilitate planning for the transfer of care.

Clearly, there is a need for training human-service professionals to assist these families. Services must be developed to support families in their efforts to continue providing care, and alternative residential arrangements must be available when families can no longer provide care in the home setting.

* * *

Joan B. Wood, Ph.D., is associate director, Virginia Geriatric Education Center, and gerontology coordinator for the Virginia Institute for Developmental Disabilities, Virginia Commonwealth University. Laura Lopater Skiles, M.S., is program coordinator, Virginia Geriatric Education Center, and was formerly associated with the Virginia Institute for Developmental Disabilities, Virginia Commonwealth University, Richmond, Virginia.

REFERENCES

Carswell, A. T. and Hartig, S. A., 1979. "Older Developmentally Disabled Persons: An Investigation of Needs and Social Services." Athens: Georgia Retardation Center, Athens Unit, University of Georgia.

Heller, T. and Factor, A., 1991. "Permanency Planning for Adults with Mental Retardation Living with Family Caregivers." *American Journal on Mental Retardation* 96(2):163–76.

Roberto, K. A., 1988. *Caring for Aging Developmentally Disabled Adults: Perspectives and Needs of Older Parents* (final report presented to the Colorado Developmental Disabilities Planning Council). Greeley: Department of Human Services, University of Northern Colorado.

Seltzer, M. M. and Seltzer, G., 1985. "The Elderly Mentally Retarded: A Group in Need of Service." *Journal of Gerontological Social Work* 8:99–119.

Seltzer, M. M., Krauss, M. W. and Heller, T., 1991. "Family Caregiving over the Life Course." In M. M. Janicki and M. M. Seltzer, eds., *Aging and Developmental Disabilities: Challenges for the 1990s (The Proceedings of the Boston Roundtable on Research Issues and Applications in Aging and Developmental Disabilities).* Washington, D.C.: Special Interest Group on Aging, American Association on Mental Retardation.

Turnbull, A. P., Summers, J. A. and Brotherson, M. J., 1986. "Family Life Cycle: Theoretical and Empirical Implications and Future Directions for Families with Mentally Retarded Members." In J. J. Gallagher and P. M. Vietze, eds., *Families of Handicapped Persons: Research, Programs and Policy Issues.* Baltimore, Md.: Brookes.

Chapter 14

'Retirement' for Older Persons with Developmental Disabilities

Evelyn Sutton, Harvey L. Sterns, and Ruth S. Roberts

The scene could be any shopping mall on a weekday morning. Ron and his friend Joe have just joined the mall walkers, a group of retirees who chalk up miles of exercise on a daily basis. Ron and Joe walk briskly up and down, exchanging an occasional greeting with someone else. After half an hour or so, they stop off at a mall cafe, joining other walkers for a cup of coffee.

Ron, a community volunteer, retired a few years ago from a local factory, where he had served in a variety of capacities for almost 40 years. Joe, who has a developmental disability, has just retired after 12 years of work in a community-based sheltered workshop operated by the local board of mental retardation. Most of his life, however, has been spent in an institution operated by the state.

The Ron and Joe mall-walking scenario may happen rarely, but it represents the kind of active involvement and everyday retirement life-style that one might wish for Joe and his aging friends in the group home where he now lives. Ron and Joe are part of the Access Project, a volunteer peer companion model that was developed at the University of Akron with funding from the Joseph P. Kennedy, Jr., Foundation. Access brings together retired senior volunteers from community agencies and churches and "retirees" from within the developmental disabilities service system to participate in a variety of community-based activities. The project provides a pathway to community integration for older persons with developmental disabilities; it has been replicated across the country (LePore and Janicki, 1990; Roberts and Davis, 1988) and is an example of the "retirement" options available to this population.

In discussing retirement for people who are developmentally disabled, this essay can only address the concerns of those who are mildly or moderately impaired and who have spent some time in the workplace, as many have since the deinstitutionalization movement of the 1970s. People who have severe or profound retardation would find the concept of retirement meaningless. For survivors in that category, very different issues must be considered.

Work seems to be the most approved concept in the system that provides services for persons with developmental disabilities. Vocational training is the main focus of efforts to provide the most normal adult experience and lifestyle for each individual, with "supported employment" and "job coaching" (in the mainstream) currently among the more popular practices.

For the older population with developmental disabilities, retirement is an option that has only recently been discovered. As increasing numbers of this special group of people join the over-55 ranks, awareness of their changing needs has gradually followed (Stroud and Sutton, 1988; Janicki and Wisniewski, 1985; Seltzer and Krauss, 1987).

However, retirement from activities provided by a local service "system," usually operated by a county, township, or regional governmental agency, appears to be quite different from retirement in the traditional sense. What is often missing are the preferences and opinions of the individual whose life is the focus of the later-life plan. It is typically the service system's professional staff who make decisions about the welfare of the individual. Activities, whether work or leisure, are initiated through an assessment and planning process, and agency priorities and associated funding limitations can directly affect the service plan.

Ohio is one of a very few states mandating a retirement option for those over age 55 who are developmentally disabled. In addition to its legislated retirement option, Ohio during the 1980s and early 1990s has been in the forefront of efforts to raise awareness about this population, train staff, and develop appropriate programming. At local and state levels, administrative initiatives have brought together the aging and developmental disabilities service systems around mutual concern for meeting the needs of older persons with developmental disabilities.

Ohio's service system for adults with developmental disabilities functions primarily through a county structure. These 88 governmental units design and implement programs to meet identified needs of their clients. Funding from federal, state, and local sources is channeled through these agencies, the county boards of mental retardation and developmental disabilities (MR/DD).

In 1989–90 the University of Akron, a site of the Rehabilitation Research and Training Center (RRTC) Consortium on Aging and Developmental Disabilities, conducted an investigation of retirement practices affecting the lives of older persons with developmental disabilities. (Sutton et al., 1991). Because of Ohio's history in addressing these issues, the researchers based their work on the hypothesis that by early 1990 a majority of older Ohioans with developmental disabilities would have the option to retire from sheltered work, other employment, or day training programs. It was also believed that they would have a range of activity choices and would have been well prepared for the transition from work to a more leisurely lifestyle. In a statewide survey, questions like the following were explored:

- Is retirement, as a lifestyle in the traditional sense, available for older persons with lifelong disabilities?
- How is such retirement similar to or different from that experienced by the general population of older persons?
- To what extent is the retirement option available, and how is the retirement decision made?
- What activities/opportunities replace the work role for those who retire?
- How well adjusted to and satisfied with the retired lifestyle do associates perceive these individuals to be?
- How do these individuals perceive themselves in this transition?

The goal of the University of Akron researchers was to obtain a response from each county summarizing the county's information about the status of older persons with developmental disabilities.

Of the 88 Ohio counties surveyed, 63 responded, representing 1,482 individuals over the age of 55. That number (1,482) is approximately two-thirds of all known older persons in the MR/DD system statewide. Two-thirds of the sample were over age 60, and one-third were in the 55–59 age range.

Interestingly, this study found most of these individuals still engaged in full-time or part-time work. Many who were working part time reportedly spent some hours on a daily or weekly basis in segregated "senior" groups, which were described as offering a variety of leisure and recreational activities.

An important finding in this study was that 51 percent of those reportedly retired or working on a reduced schedule are participating in programs at community-based senior centers and nutrition sites. Churches, parks, and community recreation programs are also utilized.

Still, the study suggests that, in many ways, life in retirement is not greatly changed for this segment of the population. Of the 595 subjects reported to be fully or partially retired, almost all still travel on their preretirement schedule to their former places of employment. There, options other than work may be available to them, depending upon priorities of the county board. They may engage in the same work routine as in earlier years, or they may divide their time between work and leisure activities, or they may spend the day in a series of specially planned activities. These activities may include exercise, discussion of current events, and food preparation. Special outings and trips are reported by three-fourths of the counties in the study.

One condition that may present an advantage for the older person with developmental disabilities is the built-in option of part-time or phased-down work. Such a choice appears to be popular in one Ohio county, where researchers found that almost all of those over 55 had chosen a slower paced, shorter workday, with components of leisure balancing their 6 to 8 hours at the sheltered work site. In many states the developmental disabilities system is well structured to accommodate this work preference. "Phase-down" and other forms of progressive disengagement from work are presently practiced to a very limited extent within American business and industry (Sterns et al., 1990). However, even the developmental disabilities system at times finds itself in the position of forcing retirement as waiting lists for adult work placement grow longer.

Researchers and advocates now encourage discussion of health status, financial situation, and activity preferences for older workers in business and industry prior to retirement (Hogg et al., 1988), and adjustment to retirement has been found to be more positive when potential retirees participate in preretirement education classes. However, the Ohio study cited above found little evidence of such formal preparation for an individual's later-life transition within the developmental disability system. In Mississippi, a retirement education curriculum has been developed (Cotten and Casey, 1990), and another later-life planning and educational approach is now being piloted in

Ohio and Illinois. Preparation for retirement and lifestyle changes are expected to be more routine in years to come.

As for our mall walkers, Ron and Joe, they show how "retirement" affords Joe a chance to gain access to community-based activities and other normalizing experiences that were denied to him in earlier years because of institutionalization and the stigma associated with having a lifelong disability. With a peer companion, the person with the disability finds many opportunities for new experience, positive growth, and friendship that truly enhance "retirement."

* * *

Evelyn Sutton is an associate professor and program coordinator, Harvey L. Sterns is a professor of psychology and director, and Ruth Roberts is professor emeritus and codirector of the Consortium on Aging and Developmental Disabilities, all at the Institute for Life-Span Development and Gerontology, University of Akron, Akron, Ohio.

REFERENCES

Cotten, P. D. and Casey, J., 1990. "The Boswell Retardation Center Pre-Retirement Training and Planning Program for Elderly Persons with Mental Retardation." Sanatorium, Miss.: Boswell Retardation Center.

Hogg, J., Moss, S. and Cooke, D., 1988. "From Midlife to Old Age: Ageing and the Nature of Specific Life Transitions of People with Mental Handicaps." In G. Horohin and D. May, eds., *Living with Mental Handicaps: Transitions in the Lives of People with Mental Handicaps*. New York: St. Martin's Press.

Janicki, M. and Wisniewski, H. M., eds., 1985. *Aging and Developmental Disabilities: Issues and Approaches*. Baltimore, Md.: Brookes.

LaPore, P. and Janicki, M., 1990. *The Wit to Win*. Albany, N.Y.: Office on Aging.

Roberts, R. and Davis, G., 1988. "Expanding Options for Seniors with Mental Retardation." *Aging* 357: 17–19.

Seltzer, M. and Krauss, M., eds., 1987. *Aging and Mental Retardation*. Washington, D.C.: American Association on Mental Retardation.

Sterns, H., Matheson, N. and Schwartz, L., 1990. In K. F. Fenraro, ed., *Gerontology: Perspectives and Issues*. New York: Springer, pp. 163–78.

Stroud, M. and Sutton, E., 1988. *Expanding Options for Older Adults with Developmental Disabilities*. Baltimore, Md.: Brookes.

Sutton, E., Sterns, H. and Schwartz, L., 1991. *Realities of Retirement for Older Persons with Developmental Disabilities*. Akron, Ohio: Rehabilitation Research and Training Center on Aging and Developmental Disabilities.

EDUCATION AND TRAINING FOR INDEPENDENT LIVING

Chapter 15

Training Families to Be Case Managers for Elders with Developmental Disabilities

Marsha Mailick Seltzer

The purpose of this chapter is to explore the feasibility of involving family members who have an older relative with developmental disabilities[1] in the case management process. The fragmentation of health and social services for older persons has been well documented (Lowy, 1980), and this phenomenon is also characteristic of services for persons with developmental disabilities (Braddock, 1987). It is not surprising, then, that when a person with developmental disabilities reaches

[1] A developmental disability, as defined by PL 95-602 (the Rehabilitation, Comprehensive Services, and Developmental Disabilities Amendments of 1978), is a severe chronic disability of a person that (1) is attributable to a mental or physical impairment or combination of mental and physical impairments; (2) is manifested before the person attains age 22; (3) is likely to continue indefinitely; (4) results in substantial functional limitations in three or more of the following areas of major life activity: (i) self-care, (ii) receptive and expressive language, (iii) learning, (iv) mobility, (v) self-direction, (vi) capacity for independent living, and (vii) economic self-sufficiency; and (5) reflects the person's need for a combination and sequence of special, interdisciplinary, or generic care, treatment, or other services which are of lifelong or extended duration and are individually planned and coordinated.

old age, the fragmentation of services becomes even more problematic. The older person must obtain services from both the aging network and the developmental disabilities service system, and these must be coordinated effectively (Seltzer, 1988). While professional case management is a useful support for older persons with developmental disabilities, there are advantages in training a family member to participate with professionals in the case management process.

The majority of persons with developmental disabilities live with their families, many for their entire lives (Fujiura et al., 1989; Seltzer et al., 1991). While it has often been said that parenthood is a lifelong commitment (e.g., Lancaster et al., 1987), never is this more true than when the child has a lifelong disability and has persistent needs for personal support. Parents are the most enduring support network for persons with developmental disabilities, as they often provide direct and indirect care to the son or daughter until their death. After the parents die, a sibling of the adult with developmental disabilities may assume the caregiving role (Seltzer et al., 1991). Even when an adult with developmental disabilities lives in an out-of-home placement such as a group home, siblings often maintain a close relationship with him or her.

In addition to direct care and supervision, a primary responsibility of family members who have a relative with developmental disabilities is service coordination. The role of the family member as advocate and monitor of services has been well documented (Fiedler and Antonak, 1991). Parents of persons with developmental disabilities have been credited with numerous achievements on behalf of their own children as well as notable accomplishments on a broader social level (e.g., advocacy that has led to the passage of federal legislation). In fact, family members of persons with developmental disabilities are natural case managers, as they have much experience obtaining, monitoring, integrating, and terminating the services needed by their relative with developmental disabilities.

This chapter has three objectives. First, the theoretical and empirical basis for the idea of training family members of older adults with developmental disabilities to function as case managers will be reviewed. Second, the results of a program of research on the effectiveness of family case management training will be presented. Finally, the service implications of this approach to case management will be discussed. Throughout this chapter, findings from both the gerontological literature and the literature on developmental disabilities will be reviewed and integrated in order to draw implications relevant to older persons with developmental disabilities and their families.

PARTNERSHIP BETWEEN FORMAL AND INFORMAL SUPPORTS

Case management is a strategy that aims to reduce service fragmentation (Austin, 1981; Steinberg and Carter, 1983; Wylie and Austin, 1978). Most commonly performed by a professional social worker, nurse, or a specially trained case manager, this function is defined as "the coordination of a specified group of resources and services for a specified group of people" (Kane, 1988, p. 5). Case management is an attempt to reach out to persons in need of service, promote service awareness, provide a needs assessment, develop a service plan, and finally, ensure that the prescribed services are received. The essence of the case management approach is to establish a single point of responsibility for the coordination of the services received by an individual. Service control is retained by the case manager, who acts as broker between the client and the service system, integrating and individualizing services and establishing an ongoing personal relationship with the client. In short, case management is a method of coping with life's bureaucracies.

With incentives and supports provided by the federal government (e.g., via the National Long-Term Care Channeling Demonstration), many states have adopted a case management approach to the coordination of services for the elderly (Applebaum, 1988) and for persons with developmental disabilities (Taylor, 1991). Case management has been found to improve an individual's access to services. However, this approach to service coordination is not free of problems. The large caseload carried by most case managers is a particular concern. In Arnold and Lubben's (1988) description of a day in the life of a case manager, the case manager worked on 12 different cases in the course of a single day. Other limitations of the professional case management model include high turnover among case managers and reluctance on the part of many older persons to assume the role of a client whose affairs are being managed. Furthermore, case management is a strategic response to shrinking service budgets, a method of cost reduction and elimination of service duplication and waste. Therefore, the professional case manager is under pressure to respond to and advocate for not only the needs of individual clients but also system needs such as cost containment. The possibility of conflicting interests and allegiances is clearly a risk.

A variation on the case management theme is the participation of family members of older persons in this function along with the professional case manager. Sussman (1976) conceptualized two roles families play in the care of the elderly—direct care provider and indirect care provider. Both of these roles are also played by family members on behalf of a relative with developmental disabilities. The literature contains numerous descriptions and analyses of the important contribution made by the family in the direct care provider role (see, e.g., Brody, 1985; Lowy, 1983; Shanas and Maddox, 1976; Seltzer and Krauss, 1989). Although the family as indirect care provider has been occasionally mentioned in the literature (e.g., Silverstone and Burack-Weiss, 1983), this function has received considerably less empirical attention, despite the fact that it is usually a family member who deals with the formal service system on behalf of a dependent relative. While healthcare and social service agencies have traditionally viewed the family as an extension of the client, an analysis of the roles played by family members of frail elderly persons as well as by family members of persons with disabilities reveals that most families, to one degree or another, are brokers, advocates, and evaluators of services on behalf of their older relatives. Although a professional can fulfill all of these functions, the history and continuity of a family member's interest in a relative who needs services enhances the family's potential to serve as a natural case manager. Indeed, Lowy (1985) noted that case management (which he called care management) is the most important care-providing function that a family can fulfill on behalf of a relative in need of services.

In a similar vein, Cantor and colleagues (1981) noted that families are often called upon to plan services on behalf of dependent relatives and to perform other case management functions. However, contemporary aging and disability service networks are highly complex, and family members may therefore be insufficiently aware of community entitlements and resources (Silverstein et al., 1985). Families who perform case management functions on behalf of older persons with developmental disabilities must be knowledgeable about both the aging network and the developmental disabilities service system, as their relative may be utilizing or in need of services from both service sectors. Hence, these families, in particular, require information and training to make them effective case managers of community services.

The concepts of caregiving stress and burden have received increasing attention in the gerontological literature (Poulshock and Deimling, 1984) and in the literature on family care for persons with developmental disabilities (Crnic et al., 1983).

Caregiving is now considered to be a normative role for adult children of frail elderly persons (Brody, 1985). Similarly, ongoing caregiving by older parents of adults with developmental disabilities is an increasingly common role (Seltzer et al., 1991). While women provide the major portion of care to their family members, both aging and developmentally disabled, the impact of caregiving on them is not yet fully understood. There is great concern among policy makers and healthcare professionals that even though caregiving has become a commonly played role, and even though it may carry with it gratifications and satisfactions, it is often a highly stressful role with potentially negative consequences for the caregiver's mental and physical health (Lawton et al., 1991; Pruchno and Resch, 1989).

In response to these concerns, a variety of strategies have been developed in order to provide support to caregivers. These include adult daycare programs, in-home respite, and caregiver support groups (Huttman, 1985). Case management training is another support that can be provided to caregiving family members by enabling them to improve their relative's access to needed services. The following section presents a description of a case management training program, entitled Family Centered Community Care for the Elderly, for family members of elderly persons.

A MODEL TRAINING PROGRAM

The Family Centered Community Care for the Elderly (FCCCE) model was developed to enable family members to more successfully meet the service needs of their elderly relative. The model strives to encourage social workers and family members to work together on case management in order to enhance the autonomy and control of the family unit (including the identified client) and to reduce their dependency on the formal service system. While this model was developed for family caregivers of elderly relatives, it is also applicable to family caregivers of persons with chronic conditions or impairments, including developmental disabilities.

Family Centered Community Care for the Elderly is a training program, conducted individually by the client's social worker, that educates and empowers family members of elderly persons. This program was developed and evaluated over a period of 10 years by professionals from the Jewish Family and Children's Service in Boston and Boston's Beth Israel Hospital (Seltzer, et al., 1984; Seltzer and Mayer, 1988). It is a mechanism that enables a family member to join the social worker as a partner in assuming responsibility for case management on behalf of another relative in need of services. The model is designed specifically for those families in which the older person is not able to perform the service coordination function on his or her own behalf because of physical frailty or cognitive limitations and is willing to designate a family member to play this role.

The FCCCE training program includes four components:

1. The expectation that a participating family member will assume responsibility for at least one new case management task to meet the needs of his or her relative in need of services.
2. Collaboration between the social worker and the family member on the development and implementation of a case management service plan for the relative.
3. Provision of written information to the family member about community resources and entitlements and about strategies for gaining access to, evaluating, monitoring, and terminating needed services.
4. Regular contact between the family member and the social worker via telephone or in-person meetings to provide consultation and to continue case management training.

The training program was implemented through individual meetings between the social worker and the family member. During the first meeting, the social worker interviewed the family member in order to identify the older person's specific service needs. Next, they met to complete the case management service plan, a form on which the older person's needs and the services that would be obtained (or modified, or terminated, as the case may be) to meet each need were listed. The social worker and the family member then decided which one of them would take responsibility for working on each task. The family member received a training manual entitled "Guide to Resources in Greater Boston for Older Persons and Their Families" (Holzman and Ivry, 1986), which contained information about specific community resources and services as well as strategies for carrying out the case management function. The social worker directed the family member to the parts of the manual that were relevant to the case management tasks on which he or she agreed to work. Subsequently, the social worker and the family member had contact at least every other week. The family member reported on his or her progress, and the social worker offered suggestions for next steps in the case management process. If new needs emerged, the case management service plan was modified, and the process began again.

The social workers who participated in the FCCCE program met as a group on a weekly basis for supervision. These group meetings began about six months before the training program was initiated and continued throughout its implementation. The objectives of the supervision meetings were to conceptualize how the responsibility for case management could be shared with family members; to review all of the steps in the training process, including assessment, the case management service plan, the training manual, the ongoing training process, and termination; and to discuss problems that emerge in the implementation of the training program. As the FCCCE model was being developed and evaluated as part of a research project, all social workers who wished to participate had to agree to follow the project's procedures. In effect, their role in the FCCCE program became part of their job description.

The effects of the training program were evaluated by means of three studies. The first study consisted of a research and demonstration project based in a family service agency (Seltzer et al., 1987). Families of elderly clients who were in need of homecare services were randomly assigned to either a training program on case management or a control group in which the elderly person received social services but the family did not receive any special training. The findings of this study indicated that families who participated in the training program were significantly more likely to carry out case management functions on behalf of their elderly relatives than control group family members. Further, in the experimental group, the elderly person remained a client of the agency for a significantly shorter period of time, with no greater unmet service needs, than elderly persons in the control group, thereby showing that the program reduced dependency on the formal service system.

The second study consisted of follow-up interviews with a subgroup of the family members two years after they had completed the training program (Seltzer et al., 1989). This study indicated that family members who participated in FCCCE continued as case managers for their elderly relatives during the two years following the completion of the program. The third study involved the replication of the FCCCE model in an acute hospital setting (Mayer et al., 1990). In this randomized experiment, family members of frail elderly patients with significant medical problems (either kidney failure or dementia) were randomly assigned to either the case management training program or a control group. Again, experimental group family members (who received the case management training) performed significantly more case management functions than did the untrained control group families and significantly reduced the case management burden on social workers. Further, there was no increase in caregivers' feelings of burden, either objective or subjective, even though they now had case management responsibilities.

SERVICE IMPLICATIONS

These findings suggest that the involvement of family members in the case management process may have three benefits. First, it empowers family members by providing information to them about services and strategies for accessing resources on behalf of an older relative. With this information and with training by professional case managers, family members can more effectively carry out the case management function, a role that they play naturally, although less successfully without special training. Second, by involving family members as case management partners with professionals, the burden on professionals who have unreasonably large caseloads is reduced. The contribution of the family case manager helps to ensure that the quality of services to the older person is not compromised even though the professional's role is reduced. Third, the continuity of a family member's involvement with an older person in need of services can serve to bridge gaps inevitably created by high turnover of case managers and service providers.

The FCCCE model is not appropriate for all older persons in need of services. Clearly, those with no involved relatives and those with acrimonious or maladaptive relationships with their relatives would not be helped by this model. Therefore, it remains the responsibility of the professional to determine the appropriateness of the FCCCE model for each family. Also, when the older person can manage his or her own care, the involvement of family members is not desirable. Nevertheless, our research in two different settings points to the utility of this model with a heterogeneous group of older persons, socioeconomically and ethnically diverse, seriously ill as well as healthy. The program was designed for use with family members of persons with chronic health problems or functional impairments including developmental disabilities. For older persons with developmental disabilities, it is particularly appropriate, as it responds to a specific set of needs (i.e., gaining access to and integrating the aging and developmental disabilities service systems on behalf of the relative with developmental disabilities) and because it builds on a specific set of strengths developed as the result of parenting across the life course.

* * *

Marsha Mailick Seltzer, Ph.D., is professor, School of Social Work, and coordinator, Applied Research and Technology Unit, Waisman Center, University of Wisconsin-Madison.

REFERENCES

Applebaum, R., 1988. "Lessons from the National Channeling Demonstration." *Generations* 12(5):58–61.

Arnold, D. and Lubben, J., 1988. "A Day in the Life of a Case Manager." *Generations* 12(5):31–33.

Austin, C., 1981. "Case Management: Let Us Count the Ways." Paper presented at the 34th annual scientific meeting of the Gerontological Society of America, Toronto.

Braddock, D., 1987. *Federal Policy Toward Mental Retardation and Developmental Disabilities.* Baltimore, Md.: Paul H. Brookes.

Brody, E. M., 1985. "Parent Care as a Normative Stress." *Gerontologist* 25:19–29.

Cantor, M., Rehr, H. and Trotz, V., 1981. Workshop II: "Case Management and Family Involvement." *Mount Sinai Journal of Medicine* 48:566–68.

Crnic, K. A., Friedrich, W. N. and Greenberg, M. T., 1983. "Adaptation of Families with Mentally Retarded Children: A Model of Stress, Coping, and Family Ecology." *American Journal of Mental Deficiency* 88:125–38.

Fiedler, C. R. and Antonak, R. F., 1991. *Advocacy.* In J. L. Matson and J. A. Mulick, eds., *Handbook of Mental Retardation.* New York: Pergamon Press, pp. 23–32.

Fujiura, G. T., Garza, J. and Braddock, D., 1989. *National Survey of Family Support Services in Developmental Disabilities.* University of Illinois-Chicago.

Holzman, T. and Ivry, J., 1986. *Guide to Resources in Greater Boston for Older Persons and their Families.* Boston: Jewish Family and Children's Service.

Huttman, E. D., 1985. *Social Services for the Elderly.* New York: Free Press.

Kane, R., 1988. "Introduction to Case Management." *Generations* 12(5):5–6.

Lancaster, J. B. et al., eds., 1987. *Parenting Across the Life Span: Biosocial Dimensions.* New York: Aldine de Gruyter.

Lawton, M.P. et al., 1991. "A Two-Factor Model of Caregiving Appraisal and Psychological Well-Being." *Journal of Gerontology: Psychological Sciences* 46:181–89.

Lowy, L., 1980. *Social Policies and Programs on Aging*. Lexington, Mass.: Lexington Books.

Lowy, L., 1983. "The Older Generation: What Is Due, What Is Owed." *Social Casework,* 64:371–76.

Lowy, L., 1985. *Social Work with the Aging: The Challenge and Promise of the Later Years,* 2d ed. New York: Longman.

Mayer, J. B. et al., 1990. "Empowering Families of the Chronically Ill: A Partnership Experience in a Hospital Setting." *Social Work in Health Care* 14:73–90.

Poulshock, S. W. and Deimling, G. T., 1984. "Families Caregiving for Elders in Residence: Issues in the Measurement of Burden." *Journal of Gerontology* 39:230–39.

Pruchno, R. A. and Resch, N. L., 1989. "Husbands and Wives as Caregivers: Antecedents of Depression and Burden." *Gerontologist* 29:159–65.

Seltzer, G. B. et al., 1991. "The Impacts of Siblings on Adults with Mental Retardation and Their Aging Mothers." *Family Relations* 40:310–17.

Seltzer, M. M., 1988. "Structure and Patterns of Service Utilization by Elderly Persons with Mental Retardation." *Mental Retardation* 26:181–85.

Seltzer, M. M. and Mayer, J. B., 1988. "Families as Case Managers: A Team Approach for Serving the Elderly." *Generations* 12(5):26–29.

Seltzer, M. M. and Krauss, M. W., 1989. "Aging Parents with Mentally Retarded Children: Family Risk Factors and Sources of Support." *American Journal on Mental Retardation* 94:303–12.

Seltzer, M. M., Ivry, J. and Litchfield, L. C., 1987. "Family Members as Case Managers: Partnership Between the Formal and Informal Support Networks." *Gerontologist* 27:722–28.

Seltzer, M. M., Krauss, M. W. and Heller, T., 1991. "Family Caregiving over the Life Course." In M. P. Janicki and M. M. Seltzer, eds., *Aging and Developmental Disabilities: Challenges for the 1990s.* Washington, D.C.: Special Interest Group on Aging, American Association on Mental Retardation.

Seltzer, M. M. et al., 1984. "Agency-Family Partnerships: Case Management of Services for the Elderly. *Journal of Gerontological Social Work* 7:47–73.

Seltzer, M. M. et al., 1989. "Families as Case Managers: A Longitudinal Study." *Family Relations* 38:332–36.

Shanas, E. and Maddox, G. L., 1976. "Aging, Health, and the Organization of Health Resources." In R. H. Binstock and E. Shanas, eds., *Handbook of Aging and the Social Sciences*. New York: Van Nostrand Reinhold.

Silverstein, N. M., Michelson, S. and LoCastro, S., 1985. "Adult Children and Aging Parents: How Knowledgeable Are the Elder's Key Informal Supports?" Paper presented at the 38th annual scientific meeting of the Gerontological Society of America, New Orleans.

Silverstone, B. and Burack-Weiss, A., 1983. *Social Work Practice with the Frail Elderly and Their Families.* Springfield, Ill.: Thomas.

Steinberg, R. M. and Carter, G. W., 1983. *Case Management and the Elderly: A Handbook for Planning and Administering Programs.* Lexington, Mass.: Lexington Books.

Sussman, M. B., 1976. "The Family Life of Older People." In R. H. Binstock and E. Shanas, eds., *Handbook of Aging and the Social Services.* New York: Van Nostrand Reinhold.

Taylor, S. J., 1991. "Community Living in Three Wisconsin Counties." In S. J. Taylor, R. Bogdan and J. A. Racino, eds., *Life in the Community.* Baltimore, Md.: Paul H. Brookes, pp. 55–70.

Wylie, M. and Austin, C., 1978. "Policy Foundations for Case Management: Consequences for the Frail Elderly. *Journal of Gerontological Social Work* 1:7–17.

Chapter 16

The Training of a Specialist in Developmental Disabilities and Aging

Evelyn Sutton, Harvey L. Sterns, Lisa Schwartz, and Ruth Roberts

People with lifelong disabilities have recently become a recognized part of the graying of America. This gives rise to the need to train or retrain professionals to meet a new set of specialized service needs. Proposals for integration of these recently identified elders into community-based senior activities have been a major factor in highlighting the training need. This chapter will first discuss the progress in cooperative efforts between the aging and developmental disabilities service systems. Second, it will describe the process of developing a competency-based curriculum directed toward preservice and in-service education for the role of specialist in developmental disabilities and aging.

The term "developmental disabilities" refers to a broad group of conditions occurring before age 22 and lasting throughout life (epilepsy, autism, cerebral palsy, etc.). This chapter, however, is confined to information about individuals and systems serving persons with mental retardation (MR), because older adults with mental retardation make up the largest number of those with a developmental disability, and also because mental retardation has more frequently been the subject of research and program development than have other lifelong disabilities (Ansello and Rose, 1989; Janicki and Wisniewski, 1985). The most frequently used terminology today is "mental retardation and other developmental disabilities," or more often MR/DD).

Those working within the aging and developmental disabilities service systems realized early on that neither group knew much about the other's clientele, programming, or service delivery protocols. During the past decade, scattered efforts have addressed this issue nationwide, with support coming largely from federal and state agencies. However, the need for cross-training that bridges the two systems appears to be ongoing.

Consumers within the developmental disabilities system—that is, those receiving services and their families—have also stated the need for trained professionals to serve the older adult newly identified as having a developmental disability. At a recent meeting in Cincinnati, consumer representatives said, "Staff who do not have the knowledge and skills to guide the community integration of older adults with DD may be counterproductive to the process" (RRTC, 1990).

Within and without the aging and developmental disabilities service systems, there has been much debate regarding appropriate service options for this special population. Is the best answer a new structure paralleling the system of services provided by the Older Americans Act? Or should all efforts be directed toward community integration and utilization of those services already in place for older citizens? As this debate continues, both approaches are being successfully implemented within local MR/DD systems. A variety of models in day programming for older participants has been developed. Some older persons continue to spend full days in sheltered work or community employment. Others choose to work part of each day, and still others are involved full time in leisure, recreational, educational, and community activities. Best practices suggest that one model does not fit all and that programming for each individual needs to be the foremost consideration, as concerned professionals strive to meet a new constellation of needs for service (LePore and Janicki, 1990; Stroud and Sutton, 1988).

In a growing number of places, the aging and DD systems are cooperating in integrative planning and programming. Advisory groups and task forces linking the two systems have organized to maintain continuous dialogue. Such units have cosponsored training events and in other ways worked together to eliminate existing prejudice and "turfism."

Supporting the integrative approaches have been agreements at state levels put together by the separate departments or commissions concerned with aging and developmental disabilities. These agreements address mutual concerns and pledge mutual cooperation and support. At present, the states of California, Connecticut, Illinois, Massachusetts, Michigan, New York, Ohio, and Pennsylvania have such agreements, and Kentucky's agreement is in the making. The administrative move toward cooperation and shared responsibility in appropriately providing for the needs of such a specialized population is significant—especially considering how limited such joint efforts have been in the past. Without doubt, the 1988 memorandum of agreement between the Administration on Aging and the Administration on Developmental Disabilities has been the catalyst for much of the raised awareness and increased action now occurring at state and local levels.

The memorandum of agreement recommends, among other things, that training be provided for staff of the two networks. Such training, the memorandum states, would include information about characteristics and needs of the older population with developmental disabilities and would also address the existing similarities and differences in the systems of service delivery.

GENERATING THE COMPETENCY PROFILE

These developments, which occurred in the past decade, have underlined the need for professional leadership with expertise bridging the multidisciplinary fields of gerontology and developmental disabilities. The Rehabilitation Research and Training Center (RRTC) Consortium on Aging and Developmental Disabilities was established in 1988 to improve the quality of life and integration into the community of older persons with mental retardation and other developmental disabilities (RRTC, 1989). The consortium includes seven universities in six states. A major objective of its work has been to develop a description of the role of a specialist in developmental disabilities and aging and to construct a matrix of essential knowledge and skills based on identified competencies.

In approaching this assignment, the RRTC researchers first convened a panel of experts to identify the tasks of a professional whose responsibilities include or are limited to the older population with DD and who, properly qualified and trained, would provide and manage the best and most appropriate services for this population. The seven panel members were selected on the basis of their recognized knowledge and their experience in such a role, and all were employed in northeast Ohio agencies serving people with developmental disabilities.

Facilitators working with this panel utilized the DACUM (Developing a Curriculum) process (Norton, 1985) to identify competencies essential to the specialist role. (The DACUM process, recognized as one of the best curriculum development methods for identifying unique training needs of specific occupations, involves the experts in listing and organizing all tasks comprised in a specific work role. The result is a comprehensive set of competencies and skills—a complete job description.)

The chart resulting from this intensive effort became the tool for development of a regional survey. In this survey, 179 respondents representing four midwestern states affirmed the 88 tasks defined by the panel in the DACUM process. They also indicated their need for training to help them achieve each task or competency.

DEVELOPING THE KNOWLEDGE/SKILLS MATRIX

From the list of competencies, now refined by the survey as well as by expert review, six experts representing the disciplines of developmental disabilities and gerontology described the knowledge and skills needed to demonstrate each set of competencies. A knowledge/skills matrix resulting from this effort was then reviewed by three national authorities on developmental disabilities and aging who were unconnected to the project. A panel of executives representing agencies serving the general population of older persons in northeast Ohio (Area Agency on Aging 10B) also reviewed the product and made suggestions, which were incorporated into the final draft. The competency-based knowledge/skills matrix now became the basis for a curriculum guide intended to serve as a comprehensive document in the development of preservice and in-service education and training for the role of specialist in developmental disabilities and aging. Such education or training could occur in universities, community and technical colleges, and within agencies.

ROLE COMPONENTS

The areas of knowledge included in the final description of the role of a specialist in developmental disabilities and aging are advocacy; characteristics of older persons with lifelong disabilities; planning and implementation of programs and activities; communication; and training.

Advocacy

It is interesting that the original panel, the survey respondents, the aging network executives, and others all saw the primary role as that of advocate. Such a view reflects an enlightened concern for older persons with developmental disabilities, who may easily find themselves in "double jeopardy" because of stigma still attached to older people in our society as well as to those with mental retardation. The ability to present their case effectively with the MR/DD service system's habilitation planning team, healthcare professionals, community agencies, family members, and others is the essence of this role. Assisting the developmentally disabled older person in self-advocacy efforts, when appropriate, is another important function. The advocacy role also extends to the legislative level because the specialist's commitment is to improve the life circumstances of those who are served by an imperfect and evolving system.

Population Characteristics

Being knowledgeable about the characteristics of *older* persons with DD, including the processes of normal aging, was viewed as a significant aspect of the specialist role by all who participated in the definition process. Indeed, the DACUM process, the survey, and numerous reviews produced an unqualified statement to the effect that everything the specialist is asked to do for the older client with a developmental disability must reflect a clear knowledge and understanding of the field of gerontology and the generic system of services for older people.

Planning and Implementation

A service plan, sometimes called a habilitation plan or program plan, is required for each individual served by the DD system, regardless of age. Regulations addressing the formation and updating of these plans may vary from state to state. Federal regulations regarding "treatment" must be observed when residential services are involved.

The specialist guides this planning process. He or she must make sure that all appropriate persons have input into the plan. This includes all professionals who have responsibility for the individual, for example, program and residential personnel, physical therapists, and sometimes a psychologist. However, input of the older person, family members, and significant others is of primary importance. Planning the appropriate services based on appropriate goals and objectives is regarded as the key to quality in the individual's later life.

The DD/aging specialist also applies his or her knowledge very specifically in designing appropriate activities for the older person. The specialist must be able to assess the client's changing functional level and capabilities as well as interests. Within the framework of such an evaluation, the specialist will find the resources (including personnel), design the environment, and in many instances create the program itself, which can include physical activity, the arts, nutrition education, reality orientation, horticulture, intergenerational experience, work, community volunteerism, or any other area of appropriate goal-oriented activity. The specialist may also design a set of community experiences, whether in adult daycare, senior centers, or the community at large.

Involving the individual client in planning his or her own "retirement" schedule is an essential skill. Counseling with the older person about options and about the future as well as the present life stage is a basic competency. The DD/aging specialist must also involve significant others, including community volunteers, in the various activity processes.

Communication

The specialist in DD and aging must be a communicator not only within the facility where he or she is employed, but must also act as such in the outside community. Working cooperatively with community agencies and organizations that serve older persons is an essential skill and requires a thorough understanding of the system. To implement community integration of the individual who is disabled, when that is appropriate, the specialist must first be an integral part of the community, with contacts among a variety of agencies, churches, synagogues, and other sources of publicly sponsored activities. Success for the older person will be assured only if the specialist is knowledgeable about appropriate and accessible community-based opportunities, personnel, and protocols.

Training

As an expert about aging and developmental disabilities, the specialist will be expected to train others who work with this special population. Trainees might include professionals and paraprofessionals in either the aging or developmental disabilities systems, community volunteers, other agency personnel, and increasingly, students in universities and colleges. As an instructor or trainer, the specialist demonstrates knowledge of adult learning principles and appropriate instructional strategies.

Recognition of the new professional role is growing, and the need for a well-prepared specialist is established. To date, it appears that no curriculum designed specifically to address such a role is actually in place. However, single modules are being "infused" into existing courses and disciplines at the University of Missouri-Kansas City and the University of Rochester in New York. Such infusion into gerontology, social work, premedicine, nursing, and other curricula represents a beginning step toward establishment of educational programs that should lead to associate-, bachelors-, or masters-level degrees or certification representing qualification for the specialist role.

Criteria need to be established at state levels to mandate such preparation. Typically, colleges, universities, and technical schools have focused their educational efforts on preparation for child-oriented service roles with special education courses of study producing preschool and elementary classroom specialists. However, in recent years, university-affiliated programs for developmental disabilities have begun to pay more attention to issues of adulthood, including those pertaining to later life. As federally funded agencies focusing on research and program development, these programs have led the way in placing issues of MR/DD within academic settings, including medical schools. So preservice education and awarding of credentials for the role of specialist in DD and aging seem certain to be eventually realized.

A newly developed matrix, the Job Training Partnership Act Eldercare Worker Training Study sponsored by the Ohio Department of Aging (1990), lists the job title "mental retardation and developmental disabilities case management specialist." Again, this represents a step toward recognition of this complex role and its qualifying conditions. In Ohio, as in most other states, however, requirements within the State Department of MR/DD for adult service personnel do not include reference to needed knowledge about older persons. Unique training events addressing aging specialist competencies are occasionally approved.

Meanwhile, within the MR/DD and aging service delivery systems, the demand for training in aging/DD grows daily. During the past decade, virtually hundreds of in-service sessions have been organized to provide a "quick fix" for the appropriate delivery of services to this population. In a few states major conferences have addressed these issues. Within the network of services to the general population of older people, some cross-training with the DD service providers has been initiated. Ohio, Indiana, New York, Missouri, Oregon, North Dakota, Georgia, and Maryland have been in the forefront of such training efforts. In Maryland, the Administration on Aging–funded Partners Project, a collaboration of a university center on aging and state agencies in aging and DD, included among its activities an internship exchange by which individuals in one "system" spent two to four days in an equivalent position in the other system, learning its priorities, program, and language. At present, Partners II is continuing the internship exchange concept in Virginia through a partnership of state agencies and Virginia Commonwealth University.

An increasing amount of training material, including fully developed curricula, is available through the International Clearinghouse on Aging and DD, sponsored by the RRTC Consortium described earlier in this chapter. A 4-page pamphlet, "Role of the Specialist in DD and Aging," and a 200-page manual, *Resource Guide for Trainers of Specialists in Aging and Developmental Disabilities* (1992), may be secured from this source. Both are products of the RRTC research described above. The clearinghouse has a collection of articles and references addressing more than 500 subtopics in the general area of aging and developmental disabilities.[1]

Training grants at federal and state levels have made possible this development of material and may continue to generate useful products for some time to come. Teleconferences emanating from Virginia Commonwealth University and the University of Rochester in 1991 have added another dimension to the overall training and upgrading effort. A major national conference addressing the broadest possible range of aging/DD issues will be held in Ohio in 1993 under sponsorship of the RRTC Consortium on Aging and Developmental Disabilities.

[1] Training material may also be obtained from the following sources:

New York State Office of MR/DD, 44 Holland Ave., Albany, NY 12229-1000.

Indiana University Center on Aging and Aged, Institute for the Study of Developmental Disabilities, 2853 10th St., Bloomington, IN 47405.

Interdisciplinary Training Center on Gerontology and DD, University of Missouri-Kansas City, 2220 Holmes, 3rd Floor, Kansas City, MO 64108.

International Clearinghouse on Aging/DD, RRTC Consortium Center on Aging and Developmental Disabilities, 159 Carroll Hall, University of Akron, Akron, OH 44325-5007.

CONCLUSION

Awareness of the group of people whose disabilities have been lifelong and who are aging along with the rest of America is a recent phenomenon. Their life histories have been conditioned by many forces beyond their personal control. Rejection, prejudice, institutionalization, and lack of opportunity for educational, vocational, and social development have been among these. For these survivors, the quality of their later lives will vary with the quality and expertise of those who provide services for them. Well-trained and qualified specialists can make the difference.

* * *

Evelyn Sutton is an associate professor and program coordinator, Harvey L. Sterns is a professor of psychology and director, Lisa Schwartz is a research assistant, and Ruth Roberts is professor emeritus and codirector of the Consortium on Aging and Developmental Disabilities, all at the Institute for Life-Span Development and Gerontology, University of Akron, Akron, Ohio.

REFERENCES

Ansello, E. F. and Rose, T., 1989. *Aging and Lifelong Disabilities: Partnership for the Twenty-First Century.* Palm Springs, Calif.: Elvirita Lewis Foundation.

Janicki, M. P. and Wisniewski, H. M., 1985. *Aging and Developmental Disabilities: Issues and Approaches.* Baltimore, Md.: Brookes.

LePore, P. and Janicki, M., 1990. *The Wit to Win.* Albany, N.Y.: New York State Office on Aging.

Norton, R. E., 1985. *Leadership Training Series Number 67.* Columbus, Ohio: National Center for Research and Vocational Education, Ohio State University.

Ohio Department of Aging, 1990. *Job Training Partnership Act Eldercare Worker Training Study Final Report.* Columbus, Ohio.

RRTC (Rehabilitation Research and Training Center), 1989. Mission Statement. Cincinnati, Ohio.

RRTC (Rehabilitation Research and Training Center), 1990. Consortium on Aging/DD Representative Participation Group, Minutes of August meeting. Cincinnati, Ohio.

Stroud, M. and Sutton, E., 1988. *Expanding Options for Older Adults with Developmental Disabilities.* Baltimore, Md.: Brookes.

Sutton, E., in press. *A Resource Guide for Training Specialists in Aging and Developmental Disabilities.* Akron, Ohio: The University of Akron.

Chapter 17

Aging with a Disability: Educating Myself

June Isaacson Kailes

People with disabilities are now experiencing problems that combine those of aging with those unique to a life spent living with a specific disability.

We have all been told, "As you get older, you slow down physically, and you can't do as many things as you could when you were younger." For most of us who grew up with a disability, who could not do as much as our peers without disabilities, this warning was rather meaningless. Others with disabilities who did listen to this warning certainly did not expect that the aging process would be accelerated. However, people with disabilities are experiencing unexpected declines in their energy and activity levels as they age. We are exhibiting signs of aging earlier than people of our age without disabilities. Yet, existing public policy and health and human services are not dealing with this issue.

When I, a person with cerebral palsy, would speak my concerns to friends who were medical professionals, I felt that my descriptions sounded vague and slightly bizarre. When I explained, "I'm not walking as fast, my balance is not as good, I have more spasticity and many more aches and pains," all I received were blank looks. I decided to

*A shorter version of this article was published in the United Cerebral Palsy Association's January 1990 Networker.

initiate my own informal survey of friends and colleagues with disabilities. My results confirmed that I was not alone.

After careful review of my situation, I decided to seek some additional professional opinions.

Because I had work experience in rehabilitation and neurology, I felt confident that I could find the appropriate resources. I was wrong! The process was disconcerting. Despite the fact that I live in Los Angeles, with its plentiful medical resources, I found doctors who specialize in children with cerebral palsy (CP), but I was not able to identify anyone who specializes in adults with CP. After a costly and probably unnecessary MRI of the brain, the advice I received from several health professionals was to concentrate on strengthening specific muscles. Other than that, no one had anything more definitive to say.

I then sought the help of my out-of-town network and obtained names of additional professionals. When a business trip took me to the city in which he practiced, I connected with the doctor whose name was most frequently mentioned. He had some very different but specific and helpful advice regarding energy conservation, exercise, and mobility aids. He felt muscle strengthening would *not* be that helpful because the unevenness in cerebral palsy comes from imbalance in the degree of damage in the brain's motor cortex. That is, the firing pattern of electrical impulses in the motor cortex is asymmetrical, and it is not going to change. Therefore I could strengthen muscles as much as I wanted, but eventually they would return to being unequal in strength. In his opinion the time and energy spent in exercising were not worth the very temporary, if any, results.

At this point, I felt I had found some answers for myself. But if I, a disability policy specialist, had to go through this rather extensive search for advice and information, I wondered what was happening with others who were asking similar questions. I also wondered what would happen to the upper extremities of others with cerebral palsy whom I saw walking so slowly and laboriously on crutches. Was walking so supremely valued by the medical community, family, and society that the long-term effects of wear and tear on upper extremities were better ignored, despite the consequences of accelerated deterioration?

CONFIRMATION AND VALIDATION

The publication of Trieschmann's (1987) important book, *Aging With Disability,* confirmed for me and many others that our concerns were real and legitimate. Trieschmann substantiated the issue that has become a reality for many of us: People with disabilities are now experiencing problems that combine those of aging with those unique to a life spent living with a specific disability.

The combination of aging and disability is an unexplored, undiscussed, and unacknowledged area. Why is this such a new and unanticipated issue? I am told that in the past people with disabilities just never lived that long, and thus little is known about aging with an early-onset disability. My peers and I are the first generation of people with disabilities who are approaching middle age, retirement, and beyond in great numbers. People with disabilities have been taught how to live with a disability but not how to plan to age with a disability or how to prevent a disability from increasing via the aging process.

Before the publication of Trieschmann's book, peer input was the only validation and support people with disabilities had to assure each other that the accelerated aging we seemed to be experiencing was something real. Her book also alerted disability advocates that we must make room for yet another issue on our already full advocacy agenda. We have to insist that health and social service providers allocate a substantial amount of effort to is sues of aging with a disability.

Trieschmann correctly points out that many of us considered our disabilities to be static (spinal cord injury, polio, cerebral palsy, spina bifida). A progressive component to our disability was not anticipated. Now, however, we are experiencing the natural process of aging superimposed on other impairments that have imposed a range of physical, emotional and financial penalties on our daily lives.

Apparently, the process of aging relates not only to chronological age but also to the age at which one was disabled. Depending on one's lifestyle, genetic heritage, and type of disability, living 20 or 30 years with a disability produces wear and tear on the muscles, skeletal system, and other body systems. Most people with major physical disabilities of 30 years' duration note some tenderness and soreness in joints, muscles, and tendons that have been carrying an extra load because of impaired physical functioning in other parts of the body. Heavy use or overuse of certain body parts (e.g., one's arms) to compensate for lost motor ability in others (e.g., one's legs) can lead to problems over time. As people with disabilities age, the physical penalty appears to increase.

THE ABSENCE OF REHABILITATION RESEARCH

Trieschmann explains that rehabilitation is not a high-prestige clinical specialty because it does not focus on dramatic new discoveries leading to "cures." Nor does it focus on the development of new procedures that "solve" problems, as do specialties like surgery, cardiology, radiology, and oncology. In the medical research world, research focused on practical issues such as helping people with disabilities to lead more satisfactory lives is considered a "weak" science. More prestige is given to "hard sciences" such as cellular, molecular, and biological research.

Rehabilitation medicine continues to focus on management of newly acquired disabilities. Hence there is little knowledge to offer the person who lives with a long-term disability. The gap between the needs of people with disabilities who are aging and existing programs to help minimize the impact of the aging process is immense. Research on "living and aging with a disability" is a very low priority! The only groups given the slightest attention in the area of aging with a disability are people with spinal cord injuries or survivors of polio (e.g., Trieschmann, 1987). What about people with other types of disabilities? Future research in this area must be broadened.

One way to accomplish this is to apply some of the core principles of the independent living movement. This movement emphasizes self-direction and control in contrast to the more traditional model in which the "client/patient" is highly dependent on experts. We ourselves accomplish service coordination to the greatest extent possible. People are not labeled "cases" to be managed, as in "case management." We are people who need to achieve and maintain a sense of empowerment in order to oversee our own service acquisition and coordination. To people with disabilities, playing a role in self-care is key. The authoritarian role of the physician in diagnosis and treatment is deemphasized. In the independent living movement there is a healthy distrust of the traditional belief that medical providers always know best. The movement challenges those doctors and other health professionals who have a tendency to be dogmatically prescriptive and judgmental in telling people with disabilities what to do and how to live their lives.

We must insist that factors that mitigate the effects of aging and early-onset disability be studied and the findings then applied. The relationship between people with disabilities and their physicians, as well as other health professionals, must become a partnership based upon mutual respect and shared problem solving. We with early-onset disability must make our needs known in the areas of service provision, research, education (especially prevention), and advocacy.

MEDICAL-FUNCTIONAL RESEARCH

Researchers and those who set research priorities must be convinced that people with disabilities are a large and growing segment of the population (because the population is aging and because people with disabilities are living longer) and that there is a great need for answers to questions like the following:

- What is the role of nutrition, exercise, stress management, and other lifestyle issues in aging with a disability?
- Does the presence of a disability accelerate the rate of aging or alter the manifestations of the aging process?
- In what way do decades of living with a disability alter the general aging process from the course it would have taken in the absence of disability?
- If aging is different as a result of disability, is the difference a generalized syndrome that cuts across most disabilities, or are there specific patterns or problems associated with certain disabilities?
- Are the rate of aging and its manifestations different for those who acquire their disability in early adult years in contrast to those who acquired it in their later years, in childhood, or at birth?
- What factors (e.g., amount and duration of extra labor, general state of health, genetic makeup) contribute to musculoskeletal deterioration in persons with early-onset disability?
- Will examination of the medical records of those who have died after living with disability show that there is a combination of variables, a pattern, that differentiates long-term survivors from those who died early on?
- Will the study of medical records, including radiological reports, and films of people with disabilities uncover short-term and long-term patterns of change?

QUESTIONS CONCERNING PREVENTIVE EDUCATION

- What proactive, preventive steps could be taken early in life to prevent or slow the specific effects of aging with disability?
- Is "use it or lose it" a sound strategy, or would voluntary curtailment in the intensity and scope of certain activities at an earlier age translate into fewer musculoskeletal difficulties in later years?
- Are there trade-offs that need to be decided upon early in life—for example choosing the rigors of walking with crutches or instead opting for use of a wheelchair to prevent upper extremity muscle deterioration, particularly if one's career depends on upper extremity muscles?
- At what point should a program to conserve energy or prevent increased disability start?
- What is the effect of exercise on preventing increasing disability for specific types of disability groups?
- Is physical conditioning more important for people with disabilities than for the general population? To what extent is a decline in energy and strength accelerated by performing repeated activities of daily living and mobility (which, for people with disabilities, are like athletic events) without being in proper physical condition?
- Does active and consistent participation in sports for people with disabilities accelerate musculoskeletal difficulties or slow them because of enhanced physical condition and health?

QUESTIONS CONCERNING NUTRITIONAL RESEARCH

- Do nutritional issues need increased attention for people with disabilities?
- Would strategies followed in sports nutrition regimes have a positive or negative effect on people with disabilities?
- Are peak performance diets even more relevant for people with disabilities, since living with disability often means continual body strain and stress? For example, those without disabilities who have been athletic all their lives and who have continued to eat properly seem to age less rapidly and are healthier than their

nonathletic counterparts. What implication does this have for people with disabilities?

- What is the effect of excess body weight on the development of increased impairment?
- Does a high fat, high protein, high sugar diet have greater impact on a person with a disability as opposed to others?
- Is calcium supplementation even more important for people with disabilities than for the general population?

ADVOCACY ISSUES

In addition to demanding attention from the research community, we must also advocate that policy makers address the following issues:

- Integrating an aging and disability focus into the practice of allied health professions.
- Reworking and coordinating fragmented social legislation that, although not intended to, keeps people poor and requires that they remain so if they expect any assistance.
- Demanding an array of community-based long-term services that embrace the values of empowerment and self-determination and that assist us in continuing to work and to stay in our homes. The issue of community-based long-term services, although frequently viewed as just a senior concern, is our issue also. If our function declines, we still want to work and to remain independent, free to manage our own lives in our own homes.

In summary, our new awareness of the effects of aging with a disability is accompanied by an increasingly urgent need for information, answers, and services. We must be heard and must forcefully demand that medical, health, and social service providers, as well as public policy makers, devote time and dollars to filling the many gaps in knowledge and services surrounding the issues of aging with a disability.

* * *

June Isaacson Kailes, a disability policy consultant based in Playa del Rey (Los Angeles), Calif., consults nationally and internationally in the areas of disability-related advocacy, leadership development, public policy, independent living center management, training, fund raising, and barrier-free design.

REFERENCE

Trieschmann, R., 1987. *Aging With Disability.* New York: Demos.

A UNIFIED POLITICAL AGENDA?

Chapter 18

Autonomy as a Policy Goal for Disability and Aging

Laurel Beedon

A worker with rheumatoid arthritis chooses to take a job downtown. This is possible because the buses that run near his apartment have been retrofitted with lifts, and his employer has purchased a portable ramp and installed an automatic door.

Even though he is unable to work because of a severe head injury from a car accident, a 30-year-old worker, his wife, and child are assured they will have basic income because he was covered by Social Security Disability Insurance.

Because of his age and the severity of his spinal cord injury, a 55-year-old man is not offered vocational rehabilitation. He becomes dependent on care in a nursing home and is unable to return to work or live independently.

With his multiple sclerosis in remission, a middle-aged man would like to try work again but is afraid that if he tries and his MS recurs, he will have to go through the Social Security Disability Insurance application process all over again. This time he might be turned down.

A 62-year-old heart patient chooses to return to work and is offered a job that accommodates her condition. She ultimately turns it down because her employer does not provide medical insurance and she is unable to get individual coverage at a reasonable cost.

Concern for a person's right to autonomy—to be in control of his or her own life—is the most basic of the issues that unite older people and people with disabilities. Autonomy is the underlying theme of the Americans with Disabilities Act of 1990 (ADA). Loss of autonomy is one of the most frustrating facets of participation in the Social Security Disability Insurance Program (SSDI).

Both the ADA and SSDI were designed to improve the quality of people's lives. Each reflects the tenor of its time in the way it approaches that goal. SSDI, considered first in the 1930s and finally made law in 1956, focuses on providing income for people who can no longer be a part of the mainstream work force. The ADA, conceived in the 1980s and passed in 1990, focuses on civil rights and preventing external factors from denying anyone's participation in the mainstream.

HISTORY OF THE LAWS

Public policy is made or changed because problems arise and opportunities present themselves. Because older people and people with disabilities share not only problems but also solutions, it is useful to compare and contrast two pieces of legislation that profoundly affect both populations. By exploring these laws from the perspective of their history, the principles on which they are based, and the assumptions they make, two objectives can be met: (1) Goals and priorities can be set for making SSDI more responsive to people with disabilities today and making consideration of an individual's independence as much a part of the SSDI process as it is a right in the context of the ADA. (2) The policy directions that made the ADA achievable can be used to set goals and priorities for the future to ensure that autonomy for older Americans and Americans with disabilities becomes a reality.

SSDI

SSDI is a disability program superimposed on a retirement program outline. When the law was passed in 1956, it seemed both logical and practical to extend the Old Age and Survivors Insurance Program to people with disabilities. For years, congressional thinking had been along these lines. A Senate-appointed advisory council noted in 1938 that "people who become permanently and totally disabled before retirement age are economically in the same position or a worse one as those who are unable to work by reason of old age," and also observed that "by making early provisions for people who are permanently and totally disabled before age 65, it is hoped that much of the pressure for lowering the retirement age will be relieved" (Advisory Council on Social Security, 1938). Administrative expedience was also a consideration: "The field organization, wage records, administrative experience, and other characteristics of the Federal Old Age and Survivors insurance system provide a ready framework for administering cash benefits under a long-term program of cash disability benefits" (U.S. Social Security Board, 1945).

This early relationship of SSDI to the Social Security retirement program has set the tone for how Social Security Disability Insurance operates to this day.

The ADA

In contrast, the ADA of 1990 is a clear statement of the rights to equal opportunity for all people with disabilities. The act's five titles prohibit discrimination against people with disabilities in employment, public services, public accommodations, transportation, and telecommunication. The law is firmly rooted in the Civil Rights Act of 1964 (prohibiting discrimination on the basis of race, color, religion, or national origin), the Rehabilitation Act of 1973 (prohibiting the federal government, federal contractors, and entities that receive federal funds from discrimination because of handicap), and other federal nondiscrimination measures enacted between 1964 and 1990 that specifically cover people with disabilities.[1]

THE PRINCIPLES

Prominent in past social policy discussions about both aging and disability are the principles of equity and adequacy: Is the benefit an individual receives fair, and is it enough? Until relatively recently the

[1] Examples of other measures include the Architectural Barriers Act, the Education for All Handicapped Children Act, the Developmental Disabilities Bill of Rights Act, the Rehabilitation Act Sections 503, 504 and 510, the Voting Accessibility for the Elderly and Handicapped Act, the Fair Housing Amendments Act, and the Air Carrier Access Act.

question of whether or how a policy affects an individual's autonomy has not been a serious consideration. Like the retirement part of the Social Security system, SSDI is social insurance in which benefits are calculated to reflect a combination of individual equity and social adequacy.

Participation in the SSDI system is compulsory for most workers, and an individual pays into the system over his working life so that, should he become so severely disabled he is unable to work, the system will provide a base of income for him and his family. The amount of the benefit is related to the worker's level of earnings and the number of years worked.

The ADA is based on principles even more basic than the need for income. Its essence is an individual's *rights*. "Taken in combination with previously existing disability rights law, it provides a sound legal framework for the practical implementation of the inalienable right of all people with disabilities to participate in mainstream society" (Dart, 1990).

THE ASSUMPTION OF ABILITY OR DISABILITY

The ADA assumes capabilities despite limitations: "Whatever the limitations associated with particular disabilities, people with disabilities have been saying for years that their major obstacles are not inherent in their disabilities, but arise from barriers that have been imposed externally and unnecessarily" (National Council on the Handicapped, 1986). The ADA assumes that people with disabilities are able and want to make decisions about their lives.

As it is structured today, SSDI theoretically encourages people to make the decision to return to work.[2] There are "work incentives" built into the system to promote this decision. In fact, however, "fewer than one-half of one percent of SSDI beneficiaries have their benefits suspended or terminated because of work . . ." (Disability Advisory Council, 1988). The Social Security–administered work rules vary depending on the specific program, but in many cases, the disincentives to work are so strong that they discourage the decision to be independent.

[2] The original legislation merely "left the door open" for an individual to be rehabilitated back into the workforce. Specific opportunities to try work were put into the law much later. SSDI's work incentives are outlined in *Red Book on Work Incentives—A Summary Guide to Social Security and Supplemental Security Income Work Incentives for People with Disabilities*, SSA Publication No. 64-030, ICN 436900.

To receive benefits, individuals must be determined by SSA to be so severely disabled that they are unable to work and earn more than $500 per month. This determination process may take nine months to a year or even longer—during which time the applicants are focused on demonstrating their inability to work. When individuals are awarded benefits, they are warned that should they decide to attempt work and earn over $500 per month, their benefits can be suspended or terminated. Should they work for an extended period, they also lose their Medicare benefits. An individual's earned income may replace the monthly benefit, but health insurance may not be available. Indeed, even if the employer has a health insurance plan, coverage of a preexisting condition is likely to be ruled out. Many people with disabilities are understandably reluctant to risk loss of medical coverage.

If, in the face of all the negatives, a person still decides to go to work and then has a relapse or develops further complications, he or she may have to repeat both the long, tedious disability determination process and the two-year waiting period for Medicare coverage. With no guarantee of being returned to the rolls, many people with disabilities feel they are forced into dependency by the requirements of the law.

FROM DEPENDENCE TO INDEPENDENCE

As viewed by the designers of SSDI, a disability prevents an individual from being autonomous. They therefore focused on replacing lost wages. In contrast, the ADA's creators saw disability as limiting some abilities but not precluding autonomy. The focus of the ADA is preventing loss of autonomy and augmenting it wherever possible.

Changes for SSDI

Some people with disabilities clearly cannot work and must depend on the income provided by SSDI. However, changes could be made in the program to provide greater flexibility and promote greater autonomy for the broad range of people with disabilities. While these changes would be costly at the outset, benefits would far outweigh the costs in the long run. For example:

- Develop an early intervention program that gives a disability applicant the opportunity to receive both physical and vocational rehabilitation at the earliest possible time. This would allow the 55-year-old with the spinal cord injury the opportunity for rehabilitation so that he could live independently and perhaps return to work.

- Establish a work incentive program similar to the Supplemental Security Income program's Section 1619.[3] If a beneficiary goes to work, this program decreases his benefits only as his earnings rise, making sure the income from work remains higher than his monthly benefit amount, and allows an individual who has a relapse to return to the rolls. The young man with multiple sclerosis could work while his condition was in remission but would not risk the loss of income if it became active. He would not have to apply again because he would be automatically reentitled.
- Assure beneficiaries who return to work that their health insurance will continue in some manner. A plan for continuation of health insurance is beyond the scope of this paper; however, people with disabilities need coverage, and most will not try to return to work without it. In fact, fear of losing health coverage is the reason most often cited by people with disabilities for their reluctance to try work. With health insurance, the 62-year-old heart patient could return to being a tax-payer rather than becoming a tax-user.

Autonomy in the Future

The passage of the ADA in 1990 was a confirmation that the direction of public policy is slowly changing from an assumption of dependence to an emphasis on independence. The ADA will of course be only as strong as its regulations and their enforcement, and numerous inconsistencies and contradictions do remain. For example, while income for workers who become severely disabled is assured as an earned right by SSDI, and civil rights have been extended by the ADA, the program that provides the income often makes it difficult to exercise those civil rights. The ADA requires accessibility to job sites and nursing home dining rooms, but personal assistance on the job and for a person in his or her home is not covered. While law emphasizes independence, physicians, teachers, older people's adult children, and the parents of adults with disabilities still assume dependence. And

[3] SSI Section 1619 work incentives allow SSI beneficiaries to receive SSI cash payments even when earned income exceeds the amount that would otherwise terminate benefits. The individual also remains eligible for Medicaid. This ends only when the individual is earning enough to replace SSI, Medicaid and other publicly funded attendant care. Section 1619 also allows people to regain eligibility to SSI or Medicaid after a period of ineligibility without filing a new application.

government programs like SSDI and Medicare continue to require dependence rather than encourage autonomy.

Further changes are necessary, and now is the time to begin. Program changes could, for example, provide access across age and program lines, thus allowing the most successful programs to be utilized by the largest number of people. Attendant care could be made available to young and old people with disabilities who wish to be in the work force *and* to those who would then be able to stay in their own homes rather than a nursing facility. Job preparation and training could be made available *both* to young people still in school and to older former workers who wish to return to work.

The changing nature of the work force and people's awareness of their own potential have made SSDI ineffective for many people with disabilities. The ADA has legally changed the assumptions about disability and its ramifications for young and old. Disability does not mean the inability to participate in life, and receipt of benefits does not mean an abdication of responsibility for either oneself or one's community.

As a society we must continue to guide public policy by demanding recognition of an individual's right to work toward achieving his or her full potential—regardless of age or disability.

In the final analysis, this is not a discussion about autonomy for people with disabilities or people over 60 or 65. This is a discussion about all Americans as they move through life and about the need for a public policy that builds and promotes autonomy regardless of where on the age or disability spectrum an individual happens to be.

* * *

Laurel Beedon is a senior analyst on the economics team of the Public Policy Institute at the American Association of Retired Persons, Washington, D.C.

REFERENCES

Advisory Council on Social Security, 1938. *Final Report of the Advisory Council on Social Security*. Washington, D.C.: 76th Cong., 1st Sess. Senate Document #4, p. 33.

Dart, J., 1990. "ADA: Landmark Declaration of Equality." *Worklife* 3(3):1.

National Council on the Handicapped, 1986. *Toward Independence*. Washington, D.C.: Government Printing Office, p. 1.

U.S. Department of Health and Human Services, 1988. *Report of the Disability Advisory Council.* Washington, D.C., p. 50.

U.S. Social Security Board, 1945. *Annual Report of the Federal Security Agency—Section Five—Social Security Board.* Washington, D.C.: Federal Security Agency, p. 47.

Chapter 19

Aging, Disability, and Long-Term Care: The Politics of Common Ground

Robert H. Binstock

In 1984, at the first national conference on Aging and Rehabilitation, the president of the American Coalition of Citizens with Disabilities expressed the hope that her organization, representing 8 million disabled persons, could form a powerful political alliance with organizations representing 32 million older persons to pursue issues of mutual concern (Rubenfeld, 1986).

A year later, participants in a three-day invitational meeting at Wingspread Conference Center, in Racine, Wis., generated a substantial "unified agenda" of policy goals for advocates of the disabled and the aging. Encompassed were issues of independence, self-determination, and dignity; universal access to healthcare; adequate guaranteed income; greater access to education and work, with elimination of discrimination in both sectors; removal of physical and social barriers to the entire community environment; higher priority for research and personnel training on problems facing disabled persons of all ages; and the development of a comprehensive community-service delivery system—including housing, transportation, attendant services, independent living centers, respite services, protective services, advocacy, and rehabilitation—with consumer control and continuity (Lee, 1986).

This listing of policy goals clearly illustrates that it is not difficult to identify, in principle, many areas of common ground in political advocacy for and by elderly persons and younger disabled persons. But, in practice, effective coalitions must realize their goals through political action campaigns that support specific public policy measures. To date, the joint allegiance of advocates for disabled persons and elderly persons to general principles has not been easily translated into a politics of unified action (see Torres-Gil and Pynoos, 1986).

What are the prospects for a politics of common ground in lobbying for or against specific policies? Do advocates for disabled people and elderly people bring the same emphases and interests to specific propositions of mutual concern? If necessary, can the two groupings modify their traditional outlooks and adopt new emphases and perspectives to forge an effective coalition for political action? A suitable and timely vehicle for exploring these questions is the contemporary issue of expanding public insurance for comprehensive long-term-care services through federal legislation—a policy proposition that has been on the national political agenda since the late 1980s.

CONSTITUENCIES AND COSTS FOR LONG-TERM CARE

The inadequacies of the U.S. long-term-care system for meeting the needs of any of us—regardless of age, illness, disability, or family situation—have been widely discussed in recent years (see, e.g., Ball, 1989; Wiener, 1990). Services are insufficient in supply, fragmented, and difficult to locate and arrange; service providers lack education and training; and the quality of many services is poor (Office of Technology Assessment, 1990). Underlying each of these problems, in turn, is the issue of financing. As is the case with most aspects of healthcare in the United States, the characteristics of long-term-care services are substantially shaped by the nature and extent of policies for funding them (see Hudson, 1990). Accordingly, success in reforming long-term-care services will largely lie in efforts to change the nature of funding them.

Substantial public recognition of a need to reform long-term care is relatively recent. The major initial impetus for this increased awareness has been successful advocacy efforts on behalf of older people, particularly the efforts undertaken by a political coalition concerned about Alzheimer's disease (AD) that began to form in the mid-1970s (see Fox, 1989). Although research on the causes of AD has progressed somewhat in recent years (Kolata, 1991), the development of effective ways to prevent and cure it is not likely in the years immediately ahead. Consequently, a major objective of the AD movement has been the provision of humane modes of care and services to lessen suffering for an estimated 3.3 million victims of dementia and to reduce the physical, emotional, and financial burdens of their families (Office of Technology Assessment, 1990).

Advocates for victims of AD formally coalesced in 1988 with the broader constituency concerned for chronically ill and disabled older persons. The Alzheimer's Association, the American Association for Retired Persons (AARP), and the Families U.S.A. Foundation (a small organization originally established to improve the plight of poor older people) formed an alliance during the presidential campaign to undertake a lobbying effort organized under the name Long-Term Care '88 (McConnell, 1990).

The next year an explicit link was forged between advocates for the disabled and the elderly when Congressman Claude Pepper introduced a bill to provide comprehensive long-term-homecare insurance coverage for *disabled persons of any age* who are dependent in at least two activities of daily living (U.S. House of Representatives 2263, 1989). Although this bill was not voted on by Congress, it was a milestone in that it was the first major legislative reflection of the fact that the number of functionally disabled adults aged 18 to 64 years who live outside institutions is more than twice the total of all comparably disabled persons aged 65 and older (Gornick et al., 1985, pp. 22-23).

Since then the lobbying efforts for long-term care that were launched in the 1988 presidential campaign have broadened to encompass the needs of disabled people and have been carried forward by a coalition named The Long Term Care Campaign. This Washington-based interest group claims to represent nearly 140 national organizations (with more than 60 million members) including religious denominations, organized labor and business groups, nurses, veterans, youth and women's groups, consumer organizations, and racial and ethnic groups, as well as older and disabled persons. One of its key legislative goals is that "long-term-care services should be available to all who need them, *regardless of age* [italics added] or income" (Long Term Care Campaign, 1990).

By the outset of this decade, opinion polls were indicating that a substantial majority of Americans—in all adult age groups—fear the financial, familial, psychological, and social consequences of dependence on long-term care and favor the general principle of expanding government insurance to reimburse long-term-care services adequately (McConnell, 1990). But, ironically, just when the principle of expanding government long-term-care insurance is gaining public recognition and is favored by many leaders in Congress, the economic costs of doing so appear to be politically prohibitive.

Any substantial public initiative in long-term care is expected to cost tens of billions of dollars a year. Major long-term-care bills that have been introduced in Congress since the 1989 Pepper bill have ranged from $21 billion to $50 billion in projected expenditures for the first year, depending upon their varied details regarding specific populations eligible for coverage and technical provisions regarding the timing, nature, and extent of insurance coverage (U.S. Senate, 1991, pp. 257–58).

Because of such cost estimates, most analysts of congressional health policies and politics do not expect a major long-term-care bill to be enacted within the next few years. Moreover, the relatively recent political experiences of enacting the Medicare Catastrophic Coverage Act (MCCA) in 1988, and then repealing it in 1989 because of constituent complaints about having to pay new taxes to finance it, have made some members of Congress particularly wary of undertaking a major expansion of healthcare benefits that centrally involve older persons (Atkins, 1990). There are some lessons from the rapid demise of the MCCA, however, that can be applied constructively by advocates who seek the enactment of a comprehensive long-term-care program.

LESSONS FROM THE 'CATASTROPHIC' CATASTROPHE

The MCCA, developed through the initiatives of public officials in the White House, Congress, and the bureaucracy (Iglehart, 1989), was the first major expansion of benefits to older persons in 16 years. It provided insurance coverage for economically catastrophic hospital and physician bills, outpatient prescription drugs, and some elements of long-term care. About one-third of these new benefits were to be financed through increased premiums paid by all Medicare Part B enrollees, and two-thirds through a progressive, sharply escalating surtax levied on middle- and higher-income Medicare enrollees—about 40 percent of program participants.

During a period of nearly two years between the introduction of the bill and its enactment as law, neither Congress nor the aging advocacy groups (such as the 33-million-member aarp) floated "trial balloons" to enable older Americans to understand what sorts of benefits they would receive through the new MCCA and who would pay for them. Consequently, when the proposal finally did become a law, there was no popular constituency supporting it. But there was distinct opposition to it from those older persons who had to pay the most new taxes and who perceived that they already had private insurance coverage for the benefits provided through the new law (Crystal, 1990; Holstein and Minkler, 1991). They were a small numerical minority, yet they were dispersed through every congressional district. When they protested vociferously against the act, Congress received no evidence of counter vailing popular support for the new law (despite the fact that it was endorsed by AARP lobbyists).

What political lessons can be learned from the Catastrophic catastrophe? How might they be applied by advocates for elderly people and disabled people in a campaign to expand public long-term-care insurance through federal legislation?

One lesson may be that in the contemporary political context, the traditional elitist "top down" approach to social legislation, exemplified in the MCCA, needs to be inverted. If a major program of public long-term-care insurance is to be enacted and is to endure, then it will probably require "bottom up" political support. The policy will need to be genuinely sought from the grass roots, with desires and demands articulated actively in virtually every congressional district. A second lesson is that the nature of what is demanded—its details and consequences—should be fairly well worked out and comprehended at the grass-roots level so that constituents, as well as Congress and federal bureaucrats, understand the legislation's implications.

APPLYING THE LESSONS TO LONG-TERM-CARE POLITICS

Although favorable sentiment has crystallized around the general principle of public long-term-care insurance, the principle masks many basic value issues that have just begun to surface in public discussion (e.g., Eckholm, 1990; Tolchin, 1990). Widespread debate on these issues will be required for a substantial proportion of Americans to understand and support the implications of any law that is to be enacted. Otherwise, even if enacted, such legislation could quickly be repealed, as was the poorly understood MCCA. Yet depending upon the identity of the primary constituency seeking support for long-term care—the aged, the disabled, or a broader coalition of the aged, the disabled, and perhaps others—the configurations and primacy of the values involved may be very different, and the likelihood of generating widespread support may vary substantially.

From the perspective of older persons, long-term care has been seen as a problem besetting elderly people, categorically. And the predominant, though not exclusive, element of interest in additional public insurance has been generated by an economic concern. That concern is the possibility of becoming poor through "spending down," that is, depleting one's assets to pay for long-term care and then becoming dependent on a welfare program, Medicaid, to pay nursing home bills. There is a distinct middle-class fear—both economic and psychological—of using savings and selling a home to finance one's own healthcare. This anxiety reflects a desire to protect estates, as well as the psychological intertwining of personal self-esteem with one's material worth and independence.

The political weight of this type of concern, however, is not substantial in today's climate of public policy discourse. Since the late 1970s, the political era in which categorical old age entitlement programs were created and sustained with relative ease appears to be over. The aged have become a scapegoat for a variety of America's problems, and many domestic policy concerns have been framed as issues of intergenerational equity (see Binstock and Post, 1991).

Seeking an alternative to the broad cloak of political legitimacy that the categorically described needs of elderly people used to wear, advocates for older persons argued during the late 1970s and early 1980s that home or community-based care is a relatively inexpensive substitute for nursing home care and that Medicaid could save expenditures by funding community-based alternatives to nursing homes. But years of studies have established that the alternatives to nursing homes are not cost-effective substitutes (Weissert, 1990). It can only be said that many older persons seem to prefer community-based care to nursing homes.

If expanded public long-term-care insurance is to be enacted as an old age entitlement, to serve older persons as a buffer against spending down, there are some fundamental issues that the American public will need to confront and resolve. Among these issues are the following: Assuming that we can improve laws for protecting spouses of long-term-care patients from impoverishment, why shouldn't older people spend their assets and income on their healthcare? Why should government foot the bill? Why should it be government's responsibility to preserve estates? So that they can be inherited? Should government take a more active role than at present in preserving economic status inequalities from generation to generation? On what basis should some persons be taxed to preserve the inheritances of others? Should the taxing power of government be used to preserve the psychological sense of self-esteem that for so many persons is bound up in their lifetime accumulation of assets—their material worth?

Widespread public debate on such issues may very well fail to resolve them in a fashion that supports a major initiative in long-term care to protect older persons from paying for their care. Indeed, research findings are even beginning to show that the incidence and prevalence of the spend-down phenomenon may be grossly exaggerated by advocates for long-term care (Burwell et al., 1989; Liu and Manton, 1989; Liu et al., 1990). Moreover, it appears that many nursing home patients who are paid for by Medicaid become eligible for that program by sheltering and transferring their financial assets, rather than by spending down until they are poor (Moses, 1990). Many nursing home patients, with the assistance of legal counsel (Budish, 1989–90), have apparently been adept at preserving their estates—and, perhaps, passing them on as legacies—while having government pay for their long-term care through Medicaid.

In contrast to older persons, younger disabled persons do not perceive long-term-care insurance as mostly an issue of whether the government or the individual patient or family pays for the care. At least as important to them is the issue of basic access to services, technologies, and environments that will make it feasible to carry forward an active life. They argue that they should have assistance to do much of what they would be able to do if they were not disabled.

The Americans with Disabilities Act of 1991, achieved through vigorous advocacy efforts, will help to eliminate discriminatory as well as physical barriers to the participation of people with disabilities in employment, public services, public accommodations and transportation, and telecommunications. But it will not provide the elements of long-term care desired by disabled younger adults, such as paid assistance in the home and for getting in and out of the home; peer counseling, semi-independent modes of transportation, and client control or management of services.

Although the disabled have advocated for long-term care services, they have rejected a "medical model" that emphasizes long-term care as an essential component of *health* services. This is understandable given their strong desires for autonomy, independence, and as much "normalization" of daily life as possible. By the same token, disabled people have traditionally eschewed symbolic and political identification with elderly people, because of traditional stereotypes of older people as frail, chronically ill, declining, and "marginal" to society.

The efforts of disabled people to advocate on their terms for governmental long-term-care initiatives, however, have made little progress. Rather, progress in getting long-term-care insurance on the national policy agenda—for persons of all ages—has been due largely to advocates for the elderly and to broader concerns about the projected healthcare needs generated by an increasingly larger and, on average, older population of elderly people (see Schneider and Guralnik, 1990).

LONG-TERM CARE AND UNIVERSAL HEALTH INSURANCE

The most promising common ground between elderly people and disabled people to further their mutual interests in long-term care may lie in a coalition for grass-roots advocacy that focuses on such care as an essential part of a full continuum of covered services constituting an adequate national health insurance program. The Pepper Commission laid a foundation for this approach in 1990 by proposing a $43 billion package of benefits for long-term care of all disabled persons, as an integral component of its sweeping proposals for reforming American healthcare (U.S. Bipartisan Commission on Comprehensive Health Care, 1990).

To be sure, a commitment to this perspective would require advocates for the disabled to tone down their traditional rejection of the medical model. And advocates for the elderly would need to moderate their emphasis on concerns about spending down assets. But, in the climate of fiscal austerity and social policy retrenchment that has characterized American domestic policy for more than a decade, those traditional advocacy approaches for seeking costly public initiatives have little political appeal.

Even though healthcare cost-containment appears to have become an end in itself, new legislation to make healthcare universally available appears to be one of the few major propositions for domestic program development that has wide support. A grass-roots campaign focused on obtaining adequate healthcare for all, with widespread discussion of the issues, might help most Americans understand that long-term care, although traditionally overshadowed by the drama of high-tech and quick-fix acute care, is an important part of our contemporary healthcare scene. As such, long-term care currently accounts for about 10 percent of annual healthcare expenditures (Lazenby and Letsch, 1990).

In a campaign for national health insurance, disabled people and elderly people might be joined not only by advocates for other groups interested in access to affordable long-term care, for example, persons with AIDS (see Benjamin, 1990), but also by other broad constituencies such as advocates for an estimated 37 million uninsured Americans and the elements of organized labor, big business, and healthcare professionals that have already declared their general support for the principle of national health insurance, in one form or another. In addition, public discussion of the fundamental value issues that underlie proposals for universal health insurance may lead us to broader ethical and moral perspectives. We may come to view the healthcare arena in a more equitable light than we have to date. Perhaps we will see that there are no inherent reasons for making distinctions between age groups, for isolating and ignoring the disabled, for separating the relatively poor from the relatively wealthy, or for treating long-term care as any less important than acute care.

Long-term-care expansion is a high priority concern of both older persons and younger disabled persons, and a relatively promising goal to pursue in the 1990s. It is only one example, however, of how the two constituencies might coalesce for effective political action. Other policy goals can be similarly pursued by translating abstract principles of mutual concern into campaigns of practical action for placing specific policy proposals on the public agenda, and working for their adoption.

* * *

Robert H. Binstock, Ph.D., is the Henry R. Luce Professor of Aging, Health, and Society at Case Western Reserve University, Cleveland, Ohio. His latest book, coedited with Stephen G. Post, is Too Old for Health Care? Controversies in Medicine, Law, Economics, and Ethics *(Johns Hopkins University Press, 1991).*

REFERENCES

Atkins, G. L., 1990. "The Politics of Financing Long-Term Care." *Generations* 14(2):19–22.

Ball, R. M., 1989. *Because We're All in This Together: The Case for a National Long-Term Care Insurance Policy.* Washington, D.C.: Families USA Foundation.

Benjamin, A. E., 1990. "AIDS, Aging, and Long-Term Care." *Gerontologist* 30:564–67.

Binstock, R. H. and Post, S. G., eds., 1991. *Too Old for Health Care? Controversies in Medicine, Law, Economics, and Ethics.* Baltimore, Md.: Johns Hopkins University Press.

Budish, A., 1989–90. *Avoiding the Medicaid Trap: How to Beat the Catastrophic Cost of Nursing Homes.* New York: Henry Holt.

Burwell, B., Adams, E. and Meiners, M., 1989. *Spend-down of Assets Prior to Medicaid Eligibility Among Nursing Home Recipients in Michigan.* Washington, D.C.: SysteMetrics/McGraw-Hill, for the Health Care Financing Administration.

Crystal, S., 1990. "Health Economics, Old-Age Politics, and the Catastrophic Medicare Debate." *Journal of Gerontological Social Work* 15(3/4):21–31.

Eckholm, E., 1990. "Haunting Issue for U.S.: Caring for the Elderly Ill." *New York Times,* March 27, p. 1.

Fox, P., 1989. "From Senility to Alzheimer's Disease: The Rise of the Alzheimer's Disease Movement." *The Milbank Quarterly* 67:58–102.

Gornick, M. et al., 1985. "Twenty Years of Medicare and Medicaid: Covered Populations, Use of Benefits, and Program Expenditures." *Health Care Financing Review, Annual Supplement*:13–59.

Holstein, M. and Minkler, M., 1991. "The Short Life and Painful Death of the Medicare Catastrophic Coverage Act." In M. Minkler and C. Estes, eds., *Critical Perspectives on Aging: The Political and Moral Economy of Growing Old.* Amityville, N.Y.: Baywood, pp. 189–208.

Hudson, R. B., 1990. "Home Care Policy: Loved by All, Feared by Many." In C. Zuckerman, N. N. Dubler and B. Collopy, eds., *Home Health Care Options,* New York: Plenum, pp. 271–301.

Iglehart, J. K., 1989. "Medicare's New Benefits: Catastrophic Health Insurance." *New England Journal of Medicine* 320:329–36.

Kolata, G., 1991. "Alzheimer's Researchers Close In on Causes." *New York Times,* February 26, p. B5.

Lazenby, H. C., and Letsch, S. W., 1990. "National Health Expenditures, 1989." *Health Care Financing Review* 12(2):1–26.

Lee, P. R., 1986. "Synthesis and Recommendations." In C. W. Mahoney, C. L. Estes and J. E. Heumann, eds., *Toward a Unified Agenda: Proceedings of a National Conference on Disability and Aging.* San Francisco: Institute for Health and Aging, University of California, pp. 125–27.

Liu, K. and Manton, K., 1989. "The Effect of Nursing Home Use on Medicaid Eligibility." *Gerontologist* 29:59–66.

Liu, K., Doty, P. and Manton, K., 1990. "Medicaid Spend-down in Nursing Homes." *Gerontologist* 30:7–15.

Long Term Care Campaign, 1990. "Pepper Commission Recommendations Released March 2nd." *Insiders' Update,* Jan./Feb., p. 1.

McConnell, S., 1990. "Who Cares About Long-Term Care?" *Generations* 14(2):15–18.

Moses, S. A., 1990. "The Fallacy of Impoverishment." *Gerontologist* 30:21–25.

Office of Technology Assessment, Congress of the United States, 1990. *Confused Minds, Burdened Families: Finding Help for People with Alzheimer's and Other Dementias*. Washington, D.C.: Government Printing Office.

Rubenfeld, P., 1986. "Ageism and Disabilityism: Double Jeopardy." In S. J. Brody and G. E. Ruff, eds., *Aging and Rehabilitation: Advances in the State of the Art,* New York: Springer, pp. 323–28.

Schneider, E. L., and Guralnik, J. M., 1990. "The Aging of America: Impact on Health Care Costs." *Journal of the American Medical Association* 263: 2335–40.

Tolchin, M., 1990. "Paying for Long-Term Care: The Struggle for Lawmakers." *New York Times,* March 29, p. 1.

Torres-Gil, F. and Pynoos, J., 1986. "Long-Term Care Policy and Interest Group Struggles." *Gerontologist* 26:488–95.

U.S. Bipartisan Commission on Comprehensive Health Care, 1990. *A Call for Action: Final Report.* Senate Print 101–114. Washington, D.C.: Government Printing Office.

U.S. House of Representatives 2263, 1989. *Long-Term Care Act of 1989.* 101st Congress. Washington, D.C.: Government Printing Office.

U.S. Senate, Special Committee on Aging, 1991. *Developments in Aging: 1990, Volume I.* Washington, D.C.: 102nd Cong., 1st sess. Government Printing Office. Report #102–28.

Weissert, W. G., 1990. "Strategies for Reducing Home Care Expenditures." *Generations* 14(2):42–44.

Wiener, J. M., ed., 1990. "Long-Term-Care Financing." *Generations* 14(2): 5–9.

Chapter 20

The Independent Living Model of Personal Assistance in National Long-Term-Care Policy

Gerben DeJong, Andrew I. Batavia, and Louise Bouscaren McKnew

The United States has no comprehensive and coherent national long-term-care policy focusing on affordable, community-based assistance for people with disabilities (Litvak et al., 1987). The financing of community-based assistance is scattered across several federal programs: (1) home health, homemaker, and chore services financed under Titles XIX (Medicaid) and XX (Social Services Block Grants) of the Social Security Act; (2) services provided under Title XVIII (Medicare) when home-based assistance is associated with a recent hospital stay; (3) services provided under Title III of the Older Americans Act; and (4) the Veterans Administration's Home Care program and its Aide and Attendant Allowance program, which apply only to eligible

*The views expressed in this chapter are solely those of the authors and do not necessarily represent the position of any federal agency or other organization. The chapter was made possible in part by a grant from the Robert Wood Johnson Foundation and is a modified version of "Toward a National Personal Assistance Program: The Independent Living Model of Long-Term Care for Persons with Disabilities," by Andrew I. Batavia, Gerben DeJong, and Louise Bouscaren McKnew, *Journal of Health Politics, Policy and Law,* Fall 1991 (vol. 16, no. 3), published by Duke University Press, Journals Department, 6697 College Station, Durham, NC 27708. Reprinted with permission.

disabled veterans. While some of these programs have been liberalized over the years, many remain fraught with assumptions and features that render them unresponsive to needs of various groups within the population.

For example, younger and working-age persons with disabilities from the vanguard of the disability rights movement insist that existing long-term-care programs, even those that are community-based, are not responsive to their aspirations for self-direction and independent living. They argue that U.S. national long-term-care policy has focused almost exclusively on financing expensive, professionally supervised services provided through homecare organizations such as home health agencies or through nursing homes (Litvak et al., 1987).

This article considers the development of a national long-term-care policy that incorporates the "independent living (IL) model" as an alternative to traditional ones. We describe the IL model, compare it with other frameworks, discuss the concept of personal assistance on which it is based, and then consider why the approach has been largely overlooked by policy makers. We discuss the extent of the need for personal assistance services in this country, present options for developing a national program based on the IL model, and finally, present conclusions and suggest research that will contribute to the development of such a national program.

We have argued elsewhere that long-term care for people with disabilities in the United States has been provided under three distinct conceptual models: (1) the informal support model, (2) the medical model, and (3) the independent living model (see Batavia et al., 1991). The three models are described and compared below, and their relationship to each other is presented graphically in Figure 1.

The early 1970s marked the beginning of the independent living movement, which was initiated largely by working-age disabled persons who sought to remove the social and environmental barriers that precluded their ability to live independently in their communities (DeJong, 1979). The movement's fundamental premise is that individuals with disabilities are handicapped primarily by barriers in their environments rather than by their impairments or disabilities. Consequently, if such barriers are removed, disabled individuals can function normally in society. One such barrier was, and continues to be, the lack of adequate access to appropriate long-term-care services for people with disabilities (DeJong, 1981; Litvak et al., 1987).

Participants in the IL movement have severely criticized the current orientation of federal long-term-care policy (Litvak et al., 1987; World

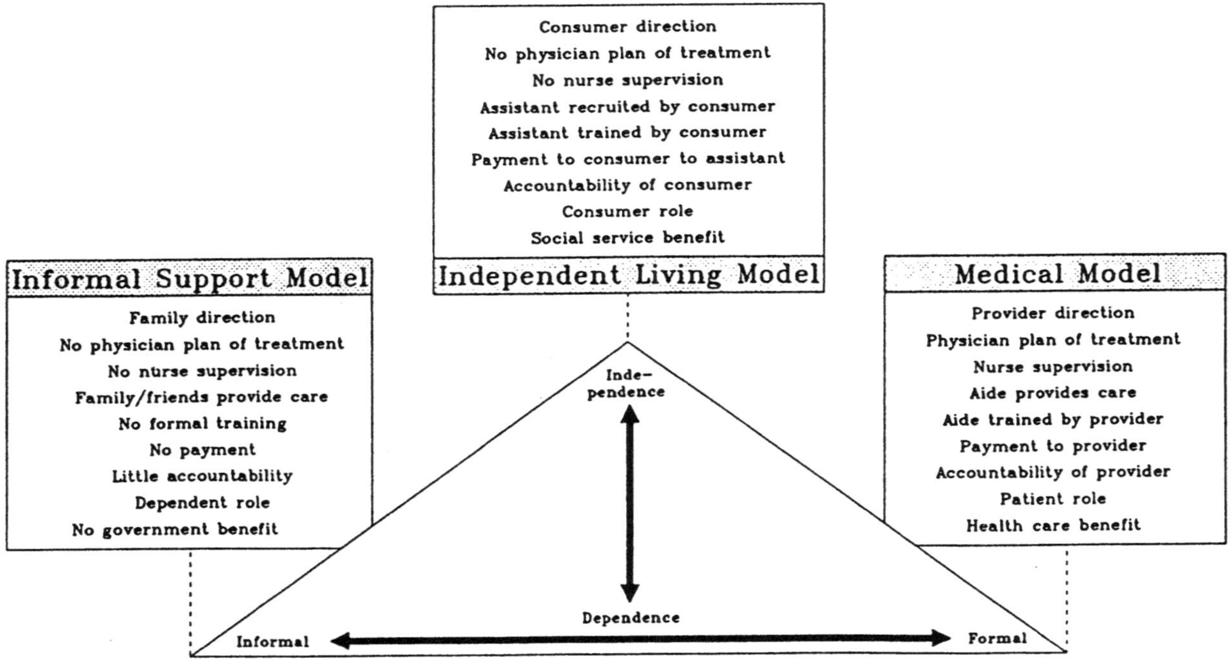

Note: This figure was adapted from a figure entitled "Continuum of Attendant Care Programs" in DeJong and Wenker, 1983.

Figure 1. Three models of long-term care for persons with disabilities.

Institute of Disability, 1988). They argue that the "nonpolicy" of reliance on the informal support model has placed an unfair burden on disabled persons and their families. They further claim that federal programs relying on the medical model are not in the best interests of disabled persons seeking to maintain independent lifestyles. The nursing home industry is viewed with distrust by many working-age disabled persons who regard institution-based care as antithetical to their freedom and autonomy. The home health industry, though somewhat less threatening to disabled people because it provides services in the individual's home, similarly is regarded with suspicion because it relies on professional healthcare providers or aides trained to treat sick patients under the medical model.

Developing a comprehensive national program to finance and provide affordable home-based long-term care in a manner acceptable to people with disabilities is one of the primary goals of the IL movement (Litvak et al, 1987; World Institute of Disability, 1988; National Council on Disability, 1986, 1988). It was in attempting to address their concerns over the informal support and medical models of long-term care that participants in the movement developed the IL model (DeJong and Wenker, 1979, 1983).

Under this model, the disabled person is considered an active recipient of services and recruits, selects, manages, and directs his or her own service provider, known as a "personal assistant." The personal assistant typically is not trained as a healthcare professional and is not supervised by a professional. In short, the care recipient is a "consumer" of services, not a patient. The personal assistant is accountable to the consumer, not to a supervising nurse or agency. The personal assistant who provides services to the disabled person acts, in a sense, as an extension of the disabled person and follows the individual's directions as to how to meet his or her needs.

The IL model is based directly on the philosophy of the IL movement, which assumes that the disabled individual is a self-directed consumer of services capable of managing his or her life. Because of the increasing number of people with cognitive disabilities (including persons with severe head injuries and many elderly disabled persons), a modified IL model has been developed to accommodate groups of disabled persons whose mental impairments limit their capacities for full self-direction (Wilkerson, 1990). Under this modified approach, a guardian or surrogate may manage the personal assistance relationship on behalf of the disabled person.

THE CONCEPT OF PERSONAL ASSISTANCE

As used by participants in the IL movement (e.g., Nosek, 1990),[1] the term "personal assistance services" embraces a broad array of activities: personal or bodily care functions, traditionally referred to as *activities of daily living* (ADL); meal preparation, laundry, light housekeeping, handling money, shopping, and transportation activities, traditionally referred to as *instrumental activities of daily living* (IADL); reader services for blind persons; and interpreter services for deaf persons (Litvak et al., 1987; National Council on Disability, 1988).

WHY THE IL MODEL IS NOT DOMINANT

Perhaps the main reason that the IL model is largely overlooked by policy makers in this country is that long-term-care policy has focused primarily on the frail elderly population, often assumed to be dependent. This assumption of dependency is not fully justified in view of the aspirations of many elderly persons to live independent lives.

The focus on the frail elderly also overlooks the personal assistance needs of age groups. Based on data from the 1983–85 Health Interview Survey, LaPlante (1989) reports that persons under age 65 make up approximately 40 percent of the noninstitutionalized population (excluding young children) who need assistance from another person in various activities. Yet, because persons over age 65 are more likely than persons under 65 to require personal assistance, policy makers largely have overlooked the needs of the younger disabled population.

A second reason that the IL model is not the primary model of long-term care today is that it surfaced as the choice among working-age disabled persons in the 1970s, a time when social policy shifted from an emphasis on expansion of service provision to one of containment or reduction of services and funding. Because few new federal programs were established during this period, the model was never institutionalized at the federal level.

A third reason is that the IL model has not had powerful *provider* constituencies prepared to work to see it funded. While it has been

[1] The term has further been defined as "assistance, under maximum feasible control, with tasks aimed at maintaining well-being, personal appearance, comfort, safety, and interactions with the community and society as a whole. In other words, personal assistance tasks are ones that individuals would normally do for themselves if they did not have a disability" (Litvak, Zukas and Heumann, 1987).

advocated strongly by groups representing the working-age disabled population, the model has not been supported as strongly by groups concerned with the needs of older persons. Although elders have many of the same aspirations for independence and self-direction as their working-age counterparts, their interests with respect to long-term care often are mediated through the advocacy efforts of provider groups. Provider groups tend to have a direct economic interest in issues of long-term care, and this interest is not well served by a participant-directed model of service delivery (DeJong and Wenker, 1979, 1983; DeJong, 1986).

The homecare industry attacks the IL approach by challenging the accountability of personal assistants and the quality of services received by persons with disabilities. According to Halamandaris (1983), a homecare industry leader, "[caregivers] should be hired through agencies who will be responsible for the training and supervision of the care that is rendered. . . . There has to be someone who can be held responsible for the quality of services that are offered. If that sounds paternalistic, I am sorry, but I have seen what happens when . . . states have resorted to the use of untrained and unsupervised individuals as providers." This position, couched in terms of good public service, has been difficult for IL advocates to refute.

Advocates argue, however, that a more meaningful strategy for quality assurance is to train consumers to monitor their own conditions and to report problems to appropriate authorities when services do not meet their needs. IL centers have sought to apply this strategy in training young and working-age persons with disabilities to use personal assistance services. Some advocacy groups now are attempting to redress the disproportionate influence of provider groups. For example, the World Institute on Disability (WID), a disability advocacy center, is striving to form alliances between the disability and elderly communities (Mahoney et al., 1986).

Despite the impediments mentioned above, the IL model has made some inroads. For example, it serves as the basis for the Veterans Administration's Aide and Attendant Allowance program, which predates the rise of the IL movement. This program provides funds for personal assistance services to qualified disabled veterans. The model was incorporated because many newly disabled veterans are young persons who seek an independent lifestyle similar to that of their nondisabled peers. Moreover, they are well represented by special interest groups such as the Paralyzed Veterans of America and the Disabled American Veterans.

The IL model has also been adopted by some states in their long-term-care policies. Several states, including Massachusetts, Maine, California, and Pennsylvania, have committed their own resources to finance personal assistance services or have incorporated IL concepts into their interpretation of the federal regulations governing community-based long-term-care services authorized under Titles XIX and XX of the Social Security Act (DeJong and Wenker, 1979, 1983; Zukas et al., 1984; Allard and Spence, 1986; Litvak et al., 1987). However, the extent to which states have adopted the model has depended in large part on the advocacy capabilities of disability groups seeking to advance the cause of independent living for disabled persons in their state.

ISSUES IN DEVELOPING A NATIONAL PROGRAM

There are a broad array of issues that must be addressed in developing a national personal assistance program, including questions of structure, organization, and policy (concerning eligibility, coverage, and payment, for example). Several are discussed here.

Definition and Scope of Personal Assistance Services

The first set of choices concerns the definition of personal assistance services for purposes of determining what services are covered under a national program. As we indicate above, the term is defined broadly by participants in the IL movement to include the wide range of services needed by persons with various disabilities. Each disabled person derives a specific benefit from the particular service he or she needs and is not able to maintain a fully productive, independent lifestyle without such assistance. For this reason, we believe that a national personal assistance program should adopt a broad definition of personal assistance.[2]

In determining the appropriate *scope* of personal assistance services, there is an ever-present tendency in this country to segregate the "medical" from the "nonmedical" domains of homecare and to segregate in-home forms of assistance from the out-of-home forms of assistance. Many disabled persons find these distinctions to be artificial and a source of frustration in their daily lives.

[2] Alternatively, there could be several smaller programs, each of which addresses a specific need for personal assistance (i.e., attendant care, interpreters, or readers).

One example of these distinctions is contained in a proposed Medicaid regulation that would have limited household tasks to one-third of a recipient's personal care benefit (HCFA, 1988). We believe that both the medical and nonmedical domains of personal assistance services are essential to the maintenance of independent lifestyles as well as the health and productivity of disabled persons and that both domains should be included within the scope of covered services under a national program.

Role of Federal and State Governments

A second set of choices concerns the respective roles of the federal and state governments in implementing a national personal assistance services program. Should the federal government be the main source of funding or should federal leadership come mainly in the form of developing national standards for the delivery of personal assistance services among the states? Or both? How much discretion should the states have in setting policies for eligible persons living in their states? How much money, if any, should the states have to contribute to the program?

We believe that an aggressive federal government role in setting standards is needed, both to address this major unmet need among disabled persons and to prevent the problem of "adverse selection," whereby disabled persons are attracted to states offering higher levels of benefits. However, given current federal and state budget deficits, it may be unrealistic to expect exclusive public sector financing.

As an alternative to exclusive federal or state funding, it may be possible to develop new and innovative financing approaches. For example, as discussed below, a national personal assistance program could be based on a community service corps model (in which volunteers are paid a modest living stipend to provide personal assistance services for a period of time), a tax-based model (in which the disabled person would receive tax advantages to compensate for the cost of personal assistance services) or a federal–private sector partnership model.

Financing Authority and Mechanism

A third set of choices concerns which specific method of financing should be used to pay for personal assistance services. If the federal government is the major payer for the program, should services be funded mainly through healthcare funding programs such as Medicare and Medicaid or through social service programs such as the Social Services Block Grants? Or should services be financed through an entirely new statutory authority creating a new program more attuned to the values of the IL movement?

Both healthcare funding and social service funding programs are currently being used in varying degrees in different states (Litvak et al., 1987). Some disability rights advocates are opposed ideologically to the use of healthcare funding for personal assistance services because it includes the "trappings" of the medical model—with disabled persons being managed as patients. While we agree that healthcare funding is inappropriate symbolically, the extent to which the medical model interferes with personal autonomy can be quite minimal. Moreover, such interference with autonomy can also take place in personal assistance programs funded under nonmedical, social service programs.

Whether the funding for a national personal assistance program derives from federal, state, or private coffers, we believe that the program ideally should be based on an entirely new legislative authority that does not suffer the drawbacks of healthcare or social service funding. Such authority should be entirely consistent with the precepts of the IL model.

Financial Eligibility and Means-Testing

A fourth set of choices concerns whether eligibility under a national program should be based in part on the financial means of the individual who requires assistance (and his or her family). There are a variety of financial eligibility options that are based on the income, resources, or employment status of the user. For example, a national program could use (1) tax credits or uncapped tax deductions to reduce the financial burden of personal assistance on persons who are employed, (2) eligibility criteria based on earned income or resources, and (3) cost sharing (copayments for services) based on a sliding fee scale for persons who are employed.

Generally speaking, we would discourage eligibility criteria based on a person's income or employment status, mainly because such criteria inadvertently tend to create work disincentives that undermine IL goals. We recommend that a national program provide universal eligibility, regardless of income and resources, with some provision for cost sharing.

Cost sharing will probably be necessary to the political and economic viability of a national program and will be valuable in inducing cost-consciousness on the part of disabled consumers. However, it should be recognized that the costs of personal assistance services are very high for many disabled persons. Consequently, cost sharing will conflict with their capacities to live independently and will deter them from seeking better-paying jobs if the cost-sharing percentages are not set at reasonable levels. Finally, it should be noted that income- and employment-based eligibility criteria are inherently difficult and costly to administer because of the bureaucratic machinery needed to implement such provisions.

Eligibility and Level of Benefit Based on Functional Status

A fifth set of issues concerns (a) how to determine whether a person needs a sufficient amount of personal assistance to warrant eligibility and (b) how to determine the amount of personal assistance an eligible person should receive under the program. This is an extremely difficult set of issues because disabled persons differ substantially in their need for personal assistance services, their living circumstances, and their capacities for managing their own personal assistance. There are objective criteria for the measurement of need, but there are few for the evaluation of individual living circumstances and the evaluation of individual management capacities.

The point of departure in evaluating individual need for the purpose of determining eligibility and level of benefit is the functional status of the person with a disability. Several excellent indexes of functional status measuring need for personal care have been developed in the fields of rehabilitation medicine, geriatric medicine, nursing, and long-term care. Implicit in the scoring systems of many such indexes are weighting schemes that reflect the minutes or hours of human assistance a disabled person may need.

An evaluation of a person's living circumstances (taking into account accessibility of the dwelling and presence of other household members, for example) and capacity for self-management requires an in-home assessment. In-home assessments should be conducted by those knowledgeable about the needs of persons with disabilities. These include occupational therapists, rehabilitation nurses, and persons with disabilities who can relate to the needs of others by virtue of their own need for assistance. At present, states take many approaches to assessing individual needs. Some rely heavily on nurses, some on county social workers. Few make good use of people with disabilities in making such assessments.

Generational Issues

A sixth set of choices concerns whether, and the extent to which, the provision of personal assistance services to working-age disabled persons should be linked with the provision of personal assistance services to younger and older disabled persons. There are substantial similarities between these groups with respect to their personal assistance needs and their aspirations to live independently and manage their own care. Thus, from a service delivery perspective, linking these groups together appears to have merit. Politically, advocates of the disabled and elderly populations have argued that each group enhances its political clout by supporting such joint programs (Mahoney et al., 1986).

While we share the view that a national personal assistance program "should serve people of all ages" (Litvak et al., 1987), we believe that caution should be exercised by advocates and policy makers in following this strategy. It is likely that politically powerful provider groups specializing in treating the elderly population will attempt to redirect a program of user-directed personal care services so as to develop an even stronger provider-controlled system of in-home services.

Training and Credentials

A seventh set of issues concerns whether providers of personal assistance services should be required under a national program to undergo a specific training regimen and whether they should be required to have a specific credential. One of the advantages of training and of requiring a credential is that these practices may encourage the development of a stable supply of career personal assistants. A major disadvantage is that trained personal assistants with credentials closely resemble home health aides employed by home health agencies and are likely to interact with disabled persons in a manner more akin to the medical model than the IL model. Similarly these assistants are likely to demand the compensation and benefits of a healthcare professional, thereby reducing the financial advantage of using relatively inexpensive nonprofessional services under the IL model.

We believe that a national program could ideally use a combined approach, in which personal assistants could opt for training and a credential, and a disabled person could choose a personal assistant with or without these qualifications. We further believe that if some form of credential is deemed essential for such a program, it is the disabled person who uses the services who should be certified by the state as having the capacity to select, hire, train, and manage his or her personal assistant. This approach places accountability on the disabled person and is therefore most consistent with the IL model.

LOOKING TO THE FUTURE

Various committees in Congress have considered several serious and thoughtfully drafted long-term-care bills and other proposed legislation addressing personal assistance services in the past few years. None is perfect, each has merits, and all struggle with ways to fund the critical needs identified in this chapter. A review of all these legislative proposals is beyond the scope of this chapter. However, we have observed that most members of Congress and their staffs have yet to distinguish adequately between (1) personal assistance services based on the IL model and (2) home healthcare based on the medical model. Both concepts typically are lumped together under the term "long-term care" or "homecare," or used interchangeably, thereby manifesting and promoting confusion. When the concepts are understood, most proposals nevertheless include both types of services in the same bill but give primary emphasis to the medical model of care. Finally, the problem of finding and recruiting people to serve as personal assistants typically is not addressed at all in these bills.

It is difficult to estimate the likely costs of a viable national personal assistance program or the current losses to society because of the lack of such a program. Examples of potential benefits not now being realized are the income and tax contributions of disabled persons or their caregivers who would be enabled to work and the reduced need for expensive forms of healthcare, such as emergency room care, hospital care, or nursing home care, for disabled persons. The actual costs and benefits of a national program will be a function of the program's specific structure, including eligibility, coverage, and payment policies. One of the major difficulties in developing estimates of the number of people who should be served by a national program is the lack of adequate current national data on the scope of personal assistance needs of persons with different disabilities. Future national surveys should address issues concerning personal assistance in much greater depth than they have previously.

Most disabled people, young and old, prefer to receive such services while living in their communities. Many do not accept the premises on which the traditional informal support and medical models of long-term care are based and do not want their assistance to be provided under these models. There is a substantial need for a national long-term-care program that is acceptable to persons with disabilities and cost-effective for society. The IL model of long-term care provides a valuable framework with which to develop an affordable national program to finance the provision of services and to expedite the recruitment of competent, dependable personal assistants.

* * *

Gerben DeJong, Ph.D., is director, National Rehabilitation Hospital Research Center, Medlantic Research Foundation, and professor, Department of Community and Family Medicine, Georgetown University School of Medicine, both in Washington, D.C. Andrew Batavia, J.D., M.S., formerly associate director for health service research, National Rehabilitation Hospital Research Center, is currently research director for disability and rehabilitation policy, Abt Associates, Inc., Bethesda, Md. Louise Bouscaren McKnew, J.D., is an attorney in Washington, D.C., and president, Independent Living Assistance (ILA), Inc., Bethesda, Md.

REFERENCES

Allard, M. and Spence, R., 1986. *A Policy Analysis of Attendant Services in Pennsylvania: A Discussion of Current Systems and Future Options.* Cambridge, Mass.: Human Services Research Institute.

Batavia, A. I., DeJong, G. and McKnew, L. B., 1991. "Toward a National Personal Assistance Program: The Independent Living Model of Long-Term Care for Persons with Disability." *Journal of Health Politics, Policy and Law* 16(3):523–45.

DeJong, G., 1979. "Independent Living: From Social Movement to Analytic Paradigm." *Archives of Physical Medicine and Rehabilitation* 60:435–46.

DeJong, G., 1981. *Environmental Accessibility and Independent Living Outcomes: Directions for Disability Program and Research.* East Lansing,

Mich.: Michigan State University, University Center for International Rehabilitation.

DeJong, G., 1986. "Needs of Disabled Persons: In-home Attendant Services." *Toward a Unified Agenda: Proceedings of a National Conference on Disability and Aging*. San Francisco: Institute for Health and Aging, University of California, pp. 46–56.

DeJong, G. and Wenker T., 1979. "Attendant Care as a Prototype Independent Living Service." *Archives of Physical Medicine and Rehabilitation* 60(10):477–82.

DeJong, G. and Wenker T., 1983. "Attendant Care as a Prototype Independent Living Service." *Caring* 2(2):26–30.

DeJong, G., Batavia, A. I. and Griss, R., 1989. "America's Neglected Health Minority: Working-Age Persons with Disabilities." *Milbank Quarterly* 67 (Supplement 2, Part 2):311–51.

Halamandaris, V., 1983. "Editor's Note." *Caring* 2(2):26.

Health Care Financing Administration (HCFA), 1988. "Medicaid Program: Coverage of Personal Care Services." *Federal Register* 53(123): 24103–24106.

LaPlante, M. P., 1989. "Disability in Basic Life Activities Across the Life Span." *Disability Statistics Report* No. 1. San Francisco: Institute for Health and Aging, University of California.

Litvak, S., Zukas, H. and Heumann, J. E., 1987. *Attending to America: Personal Assistance for Independent Living*. Berkeley, Calif.: World Institute on Disability.

Mahoney, C. W., Estes, C. L. and Heumann, J. E., 1986. *Toward a Unified Agenda: Proceedings of a National Conference on Disability and Aging*. San Francisco: Institute For Health and Aging, University of California.

McKnew, L., 1989. "A National Crisis—A National Chance: The Elderly, the Handicapped, and the 'Citizen Corps.' " Baltimore, Md.

National Council on Disability, 1986. *Toward Independence*. Washington, D.C.

National Council on Disability, 1988. *On the Threshold of Independence*. Washington, D.C.

Nosek, M., 1990. *Personal Assistance Services: A Review of Literature and Analysis of Policy Implications*. Houston, Tex.: Independent Living Resource Utilization.

Parsons, T., 1951. *The Social System*. Glencoe, Ill.: Free Press, pp. 428–79.

Pepper Commission, 1990. *Recommendations to the Congress by The Pepper Commission, U.S. Bipartisan Commission on Comprehensive Health Care—Access to Health Care and Long-Term Care for All Americans*. Washington, D.C.: Government Printing Office.

Wilkerson, D., 1990. *Independent Living Services to People with Traumatic Brain Injury: Can IL Centers Fill the Gap?* Houston, Tex.: Independent Living Resource Utilization.

World Institute of Disability, 1988. *A Report to the National Council on the Handicapped on Measures of Promoting Personal Assistance Services for People With Disabilities*. Berkeley, Calif.: World Institute on Disability.

Zukas, H., Cone, K. and Leon, J., 1984. *Descriptive Analysis of the In-Home Supportive Services Program in California*. Berkeley, Calif.: World Institute on Disability.

Chapter 21

Changing Complex Long-Term-Care Systems

Kay Charron

Vermont is working to change its long-term-care system serving persons from both aging and disability populations. There is a need to consolidate a fragmented delivery system, expand in-home services enabling persons to remain independent, and move toward a value-based service system that reflects the importance of individuality, self-sufficiency, and community association. But a decade of discussions and long-term-care studies still leaves us with an approach to long-term care that is biased in favor of institutions and with services that predominantly address functional limitations while ignoring quality of life. We are still left with a system that stigmatizes those using it and and isolates them from their own neighbors and community. We are still left with a system that threatens individual choice and power to direct one's own life.

How does fundamental change to a complex service system take place? If we look at any significant social change, we see common elements that are prerequisites:

1. Dissatisfaction with what is—reaching a point of collective intolerance with the status quo.
2. Paradigm shift—adopting new beliefs that create new possibilities.
3. Willingness to experiment—having courage to make mistakes.

4. Building strong coalitions of support—joining with others as agents of change.

DISSATISFACTION WITH WHAT IS

The fundamental inadequacy of current long-term-care systems can be truly experienced only at the individual human level. We need to get beyond system management perspectives and reconnect to the daily lives of individuals needing support with independent living. We must stop looking at actuarial data and spend time with individuals in their homes and in their daily-living patterns, so that we come to know their fears, their frustrations, their dreams, their self-images, their capabilities, their life values, their limitations, their families. Providers who say "it's not broke, so why fix it" and claim that more money would solve all the problems have probably not sat at a kitchen table with a frail elder or a brain-injured individual in a long time, if ever. We can list system problems—needed services not available, inequitable access, poor information and referral, inadequate assessment and care planning, inflexible service methods that conflict with lifelong preferences, and the like. But we need to experience the pain of the affected persons daily reality. Only by taking our own protective shields down will we reach a collective point of intolerance with existing long-term-care systems. When we share these others' lives and recognize our sameness, we will not accept the system for them any more than we would accept it for ourselves.

PARADIGM SHIFT

A paradigm is a pattern of thinking drawn from a set of assumptions or beliefs. Together these beliefs define our expectations of what is possible or acceptable. In other words, our paradigms reflect our point of view, our perception. What we see and what we screen out is largely determined by our paradigms. What does this have to do with changing a complex long-term-care system? For change to occur, one has to be willing to let new information in that one has been unconsciously screening out—information inconsistent with or alien to our prevailing "acceptable" way of doing things.

When the human-service business began about a hundred years ago, it reflected then-prominent theories and assumptions about assistance to others. The fact that these were not necessarily fully articulated did not make them any less influential in shaping the character of human services. Human-service practices still reflect a dated paradigm based on the following notions about people who need services and about how those services should be rendered:

1. *Deficiency.* People who need services are incapable, retarded, dumb, demented, crippled.
2. *Survival.* The best we can hope for for persons served is to minimize pain and meet their basic physical needs.
3. *Segregation.* We should remove persons needing services from society—institutionalize them.
4. *Protection.* Save these poor people from harm and protect our communities from damage these people might do.
5. *Professionalization.* Others should decide and control the lives of persons needing services.
6. *Dependence.* Persons requiring service need to be taken care of—welfare.

Whether we like to see it or not, every human-service program can find remnants of the above imbedded in its policies and practices even today. Broad social paradigms change slowly. In 1776 we gave up the paradigm of aristocracy and declared that all men are created equal, yet it took almost another hundred years before we abolished slavery and another century before the 1960s saw the civil rights movement. In the early 1970s, human services worked to de-institutionalize patients, but often we simply created smaller institutions called group homes. The paradigm of deficiency, survival, segregation, protection, professionalization, and dependence had not changed. For the most part, we just changed the location of service. The goal to integrate individuals into the community was not fully reached. But these early steps have led Vermont to today's challenge of developing a community-integrated independent-living system.

We have a greater chance of success today because we can choose to embrace a new paradigm. Our old beliefs have not led us to a desired destination. Now is the time to replace them with new ones (see Table 1).

WILLINGNESS TO EXPERIMENT

As with personal changes in our lives, system changes are also accompanied by a mix of feelings: being lost or confused, feelings of excitement, determination, and creative daring. We are not sure how

Table 1. Shifting Paradigm for Human Services

Old	New
deficiency	capability
survival	happiness/success
segregation	community/relationship
protection	opportunity
professionalization	choice
dependence	independence

our new future can be shaped, but somehow we must muddle through each day making choices more on intuition than on logic. When one choice doesn't work, we need to adjust and keep moving toward the future we are searching for. As we shift from an old paradigm of long-term care to a new one of independent living, we must be willing to experiment.

Vermont is assembling consumers and providers to explore creatively the desired characteristics of an independent living system. Through grass-roots planning, interested Vermont citizens are working with state policy makers to define the character and service methods wanted for Vermont's Independent Living System. We have yet to build consensus around answers, but we do have real people discussing the right questions. We are building a vision for change.

Questions being asked include the following: What might residential-care homes look like in the new paradigm? Could we create apartment units where persons could retain their own possessions and privacy while still having access to a wide variety of supported-living services that individuals could draw on according to their own needs? Could we do away with care levels for facilities so that an individual's residence is not threatened as his care needs change? What would hospital discharge planning look like in the new paradigm? Could community volunteers be trained to offer assistance to discharged persons who live alone? Could nursing homes provide short-term postacute care at a person's home with a strong rehabilitation/home adaptation focus enabling self-sufficiency in just weeks or months? How could we design independent living services so that persons have maximum opportunity to strengthen relationships with people living in their own community? How can we support individuals with functional limitations to use their capabilities to contribute to others? How might we design services to strengthen self-esteem? How could more income-producing opportunities be made available to persons with functional limitations? Is it possible to design an independent living system so that services are created for each individual's needs and circumstances rather than establishing generic service programs that people are forced to fit into? What support and incentives can we provide informal caregivers? How can we get the system to put more emphasis on the social and emotional dimensions of independent living?

To find answers to these questions, we must be willing to do more than tinker with existing programs. We must be willing to look at the policies and practices at the foundation of our present system. We must be willing to explore and adopt new service methods that no one can even visualize today.

BUILDING COALITIONS

To replace long-term care with a new independent-living service system, it is time for the fields of aging and disabilities to join in partnership. Likewise, it is time for consumers and providers to join in partnership. Only in partnership can we decide if we have reached a level of dissatisfaction compelling us to change. Only in partnership can we create a new paradigm for independent living. And only in partnership can we creatively experiment with better ways to support individuals to live satisfying and independent lives. We must bring a strong and diverse constituency together—and it must be a constituency of equals. This constituency would have two important goals. It would design and build a new system of services for independent living. And it would work politically to alter the public policy and funding biases that hold the current, unwanted long-term-care system in place. We cannot accept policies that dictate service methods at the expense of individual choice. We cannot accept policies that reimburse for services delivered in institutional settings but not in community/in-home settings. We cannot accept policies that give priority to physical needs at the expense of quality of life. We cannot accept policies that support the old paradigm while blocking progress on the new. Only by speaking in a collective voice will we have the power to demand the system changes that are truly in the best interest of us all. Vermont is beginning such a coalition-building process in 1992. We will work throughout the year to redesign our long-term-care system and hope to replace it with a new paradigm of a community-assisted independent living system.

* * *

Kay Charron is senior policy analyst, Vermont Department of Aging and Disabilities, Waterbury.

For Product Safety Concerns and Information please contact our EU representative GPSR@taylorandfrancis.com
Taylor & Francis Verlag GmbH, Kaufingerstraße 24, 80331 München, Germany

www.ingramcontent.com/pod-product-compliance
Ingram Content Group UK Ltd.
Pitfield, Milton Keynes, MK11 3LW, UK
UKHW021502240926
475702UK00035B/160

* 9 7 8 0 4 1 5 7 8 5 1 5 0 *